Like a
Library
Burning
Sharing and Saving a Lifetime of Stories

By Scott Farnsworth and Peggy R. Hoyt

LIKE A LIBRARY BURNING

Sharing and Saving a Lifetime of Stories

ISBN *0-9719177-7-9*

Published by Legacy Planning Partners, LLC
254 Plaza Drive
Oviedo, Florida 32765
Phone (407) 977-8080
Facsimile (407) 977-8078
www.BeAnAuthor.com

DEDICATION

This book is dedicated to our fathers, Marion Farnsworth

and John Hoyt, whose stories through the years have guided us,

instructed us, corrected us, and inspired us. We thank you both

for living lives "worth the writing."

We also dedicate this book to the exceptional men and women of the

SunBridge Legacy Builder Network, an organization of professional

advisors committed to touching hearts, connecting families, and changing

lives through story-based planning. We invite you to find one in

your area at www.CertifiedLegacyAdvisor.com, *or to learn*

how to become one at www.SunBridgeLegacy.com

For more information or to order a copy of this book,
visit **www.LikeALibraryBurning.com**
or call **407.977.8080** or **407.593.2386**

Book Design by Julie Hoyt Dorman
www.dormangraphics.com

TABLE OF CONTENTS

FORWARD

As a reporter who has covered personal finance for 25 years, I was curious when a source told me about a new kind of financial and estate planning that was being taught to advisors by Scott Farnsworth. Always a cynic, I didn't really believe there could be much new about the subject.

But I followed up and contacted Scott because I had developed a pressing personal interest in estate planning. I was about to turn 52, and my wife Mindy and I had no wills to protect our two children, Alison, 15, and Jason, 13. I called Scott and asked him to let me put his ideas to a real test: try his approach with my wife, Mindy. Scott agreed.

A few days later, I called Scott with my wife on the line. I stayed silent and listened while Scott went through one of his Priceless Conversations with Mindy. I'll never forget what happened during that 45-minute phone call. Scott engaged my wife in a conversation about how we could pass our values, our faith, and our heritage along with our financial assets to Alison and Jason. By the end of the call, Mindy was in tears and I was emotionally shaken.

A few months earlier, Mindy and I had worked with a prominent estate planner who wrote our wills. But the 100-page document sat in a pile of paperwork in our kitchen. Mindy and I had allowed our wills to sit for months unsigned. Why didn't we just sign them and send them back to the attorney? How could we be so irresponsible? After Scott's conversation with Mindy, the answer was clear. While our wills contained all of the right legal remedies—trusts that could protect our kids from themselves, creditors and the IRS, they lacked the personal connection we wanted to feel. They failed to give voice to our greatest hopes for our children.

People have a natural desire to pass on more to loved ones than their money. Our humanity instills in us a need to help the next generation progress by passing on what we have learned, the ideas we hold most dear, and beliefs precious to us. Traditional estate planning fails to address this most fundamental desire. As a result, many wills go unsigned, and many people die without ever passing on their most valuable assets. Wisdom is wasted, like a library burned.

The effort to prevent this sin of wasting mankind's fuel—our knowledge—is a noble one, but it surely will not be easy. The financial and estate planning industry is an entrenched, complex system with established financial incentives, professional roles, and educational infrastructure. Changing the established financial and estate planning system requires changing the way lawyers, insurance agents, and financial advisors think, and changing the way clients think. Though it may take five, 10, or 20 years, financial and estate planning will change and adopt the ideas laid out in this book because clients and good professionals will demand it.

This type of caring, probing, and personal planning—let's call it story-based planning—will ultimately become the norm for practitioners because it is good for people, makes the world better, and makes our lives more meaningful. It is progress. And this book is a first major step toward reaching this worthy goal.

—Andrew Gluck
President & CEO, Advisor Products Inc.
Editor-at-Large, Financial Advisor Magazine
www.advisorproducts.com
www.fa-mag.com

INTRODUCTION

"WHEN AN OLD PERSON DIES,

IT'S LIKE A LIBRARY BURNING DOWN."

—MIDDLE EASTERN PROVERB

This proverb may have had its historical origins in the story of the Library at Alexandria, Egypt. For several centuries it was the crown jewel of the Western intellectual world. At its height, it maintained an incomparable collection of an estimated 700,000 scrolls containing a vast store of the knowledge and wisdom of our civilization.

It would be difficult to overstate its importance. The library was open to students from all cultures, and many travelled to Alexandria and became permanent residents. As a result, the library became as renowned for the studies it supported as for its collection. Achievements of scholars working there include the translation of the Bible from Hebrew to Greek; the calculation of the shape and size of the earth and the relationship of the sun and the solar system; the development of a comprehensive atlas of the stars; the invention of library science; the creation of geometry; and important advances in anatomy and medicine.

The library stood for 300 years until a fire destroyed most of its main premises during Julius Caesar's conquest in 48 B.C. The main branch was completely destroyed along with the entire royal quarter of the city during the campaign of Aurelius in 272 A.D. A smaller branch survived until 391 A.D., when the bishop of Alexandria burned it to the ground.

It is staggering to contemplate the vast amount of information, knowledge, and wisdom that were destroyed along with this facility. Who can imagine the number of scientific breakthroughs, historical insights, and philosophical understandings that were delayed for centuries—or lost forever—because of these fires? Clearly, the world is poorer today because of this tragedy.

Similar losses have occurred throughout recorded history. For example, in 16th Century Mexico, the conquering Spaniards obliterated nearly all of the Mayan codices, thus rubbing out the highly advanced learning of the Mayans in astronomy, art, mathematics, architecture, calendaring, and horticulture. In 1908, fire destroyed part of the library at Johns Hopkins University in Baltimore, causing what authorities described as "inestimable damage." Unless precautionary action is taken, fires, floods, and earthquakes can destroy in a moment what has taken decades or centuries to accumulate.

But as tragic as these losses were, we believe similar tragedies—though largely unnoticed—are happening all around us every day. To paraphrase the proverb, **when any one of us—young or old—dies without sharing and saving our stories, it's like a library burning down.**

Each of us is a library, a living depository of vast amounts of knowledge, information, wisdom, insight, and life-lessons. Within us we hold countless treasures: stories, memories, eye-witness accounts, compilations of decades of personal experiences. This human wealth is profoundly valuable and intensely fragile. It can be easily lost to death, disease, dementia, or any of a dozen other causes. Unless thoughtful steps are taken beforehand to preserve and pass it on, it will be destroyed and lost forever.

To let this happen would be a tragedy of the first magnitude. We must act with urgency to avert this disaster. We must not let the library—any library—burn down. We must find ways to share and save a lifetime of stories. ∞

CHAPTER 1

LEGACY STORIES

"THE GREATEST SECRETS ARE
ALWAYS HIDDEN IN THE MOST UNLIKELY PLACES.
THOSE WHO DON'T BELIEVE IN MAGIC
WILL NEVER FIND IT."
— ROALD DAHL

The artifacts of human life are precariously fragile. Significant treasures can be lost forever, sometimes with little or no warning. Whether by natural causes or man-made disasters, precious relics created over years or decades or even centuries can vanish in a moment. Sometimes these losses affect whole countries or continents; sometimes they are intimate and personal. In every case, we are left impoverished as a result.

Scott's family has no pictures of him as a baby or young child because all their photographs were destroyed when their house burned down when he was three years old. He shares this story:

One of my very earliest memories is of my brothers and mother and me running from the house and down the front sidewalk barefoot in our pajamas in the middle of the night, my mother telling us to hurry and not look back. My father had come home from a late-night church meeting and discovered the house already well ablaze. He woke us and got us out of the house, then stayed to fight the fire with the help of his brother and a few neighbors.

I remember waiting for what seemed an eternity at my uncle's house half a mile away, whimpering and worrying about the well-being of my father and my toys and clothes in the midst of that fire. I remember the mix of emotions I felt when my father finally joined us. As my mother rubbed butter on his burned hands and combed out his singed hair, he told us how he had discovered the fire and woke us up and got us to safety, but then struggled in vain to control the blaze and save the house and our possessions. By the time the local volunteer fire department had arrived with their truck, it was too late. It was a total loss. All my toys and clothes and even my shoes were gone. (I learned many years later that due to a mistake by the insurance agent, the house and all its contents were uninsured, so the loss was indeed "total.")

I remember how depressing it was to go back to the still-smoldering house the next day. I remember the smell and the smoky blackness covering everything. I remember picking through the ashes trying to find something, anything, that was still usable or even recognizable. I remember finding a few mostly-whole cedar shake shingles and suggesting that maybe we could use them when we built a new house.

Fortunately, no one died or was seriously injured in that fire. We lost our house and our possessions, but the people were safe. The greater disaster had been avoided, and the events of that tragic evening would become another volume in our family's library of legacy stories.

When pressed, my dad would occasionally tell that story over the years. He would share it on long drives, sitting around the campfire on fishing trips, and during family reunions. Interestingly, as he told it, it was not a story of loss or victimhood. Instead, it was a story of divine intervention—of leaving the meeting earlier than usual that night and coming straight home, arriving just in time to rescue his family from the fire. It was a story of neighborly kindness—of relatives and neighbors and church friends coming to the aid of a young farm family who had lost everything, providing them clothes, toys, dishes, and a place to live while they rebuilt their home and their lives. It was a story of choosing your own attitude in the face of hardship—of not blaming insurance agents or others but picking yourself up and going forward, playing the hand life deals you with courage and faith.

Fortunately, my dad lived 53 more years after that fateful fire and in that time he experienced a vast collection of additional legacy stories, many of which he shared and we were able to save. In many ways, his was an unremarkable life, but in others it was exceptional and extraordinary. He never had nor left behind much money, but he did leave a vast treasure house of wisdom and experiences which over the years will pay his posterity rich dividends. Shortly after he died in the summer of 2007, I sent this brief message to my professional colleagues:

> *Dear Friends,*
>
> *I know many of you have been following my dad's progress fighting multiple myeloma. We thought he was doing better, although he always had serious and constant pain. He went back into the hospital (which he hated with a passion) over the weekend with blood in his urine and so much pain he could not take his medicine. Late Monday evening he passed away. His services will be this Saturday in Fruitland, New Mexico.*
>
> *The library is now permanently closed but fortunately we retrieved many of the volumes before the doors were locked. He was an enthusiastic and cooperative beta-tester for many of my Legacy Builder concepts, so his story will long be told and heard and read and remembered. I will miss him deeply, as will his wife Lucile, 12 surviving children, 44 grandchildren, and a vast array of great-grandchildren. Thank you for your prayers on our behalf.*
>
> *—Scott*

Peggy also has a wonderful father. He was a minister during much of her childhood and then became president of The Humane Society of the United States. She shares this story:

Growing up, I always remembered my Dad saying that he was going to write a book called, *Letters to My Children.* As a child, I thought this sounded like a great book and a great idea. I wanted to read this book to see what my Dad had to say to me, one of his children. As time went on, life got busy and my Dad never got around to writing his book. But I never forgot and I would encourage my Dad from time to time to please write his book, my book, the one he was writing for me.

Many years later, I decided to write a book of my own. This was the perfect opportunity for my Dad, I thought. I said, "Dad, you write your book and I'll write mine and we'll see who finishes first." I felt certain this would be enough to get him moving forward. Still, no book and I remained disappointed, afraid that something would happen to my Dad and I would never have the chance to read the book that was meant for me.

Finally, in frustration, I asked my Dad, who had been a prolific writer and speaker all of his professional career, if he would be willing to gather up some of the things he had written—poems, letters, sermons and speeches. He agreed and chose those things that had the most meaning for him. Now I had something to work with—content for a book, written by my Dad.

Upon reviewing the items he sent, I discovered a poem entitled, *"I Live but Once."*

I LIVE BUT ONCE

I live but once, so live I must
That life may be no dream denied,
No vision without birth
Upon the horizon of a well-meaning
    tomorrow.

My life is this moment, this brief incident
    of consciousness
When those years which were not mine
    to choose
Define the limits of my awareness.

I live but once, so live I must
To bring forth that endowment which is mine to
    give;
That small portion of life's spirit which,
    once the seed of my birth,
Becomes now the bequest of my living.

I live, therefore, conscious of all this moment
    demands,
Knowing not when it will end, only that it has
    begun;
And that I, whoever I am,
Possess the potential to make it blessed
    or cursed.

I live but once, so live I must
As if life's challenge were mine alone;
No one else to assume the task given me,
No one else to fill the void of my demise.

Grant me to live, therefore,
That the measure of my life may weight the balance
   for good,
That the landscape of my existence shall nurture val-
   ues of right,
And the brightness of my days overcome the darkness
   of my nights.

I live but once, so live I must
That this life may in the future of God's intention
Be fulfilled in the grace of his love;
And this once upon a time when I lived become an
   eternity which never dies.

   —*John A. Hoyt 12/9/67*

After reading the poem, I thought this would be the perfect title for my Dad's book. Fortunately, my sister Julie is a graphic designer. So we combined our efforts—mine at compiling and editing, hers at designing. Finally, after years of waiting, we had our book. We presented our Dad with "his book" at my parents' fiftieth wedding anniversary. He was so happy and proud—you would have thought the book was on the bestseller's list. He gave one to our Mom and to each of the children – each autographed with a personal inscription.

I will always cherish my Dad's book. It holds special meaning for me in many ways. Thankfully he's still with us, but when the day comes that he's gone, we won't be wishing we had made this dream come true.

Many families are not so fortunate. When one of their loved ones dies, has a stroke, or suffers a debilitating form of dementia, the family has not preserved their legacy stories and passed them forward to future generations. The family can't hear the sounds of their loved one's laughter or share the stories of their childhood, their courtship and marriage, or their favorite recipes and vacations. The family has lost forever their parent or grandparent's expressions of love, of religious faith, of advice on how to build a strong family or survive a terrible loss. The family has photographs, but not the stories that make those pictures speak. The family has pocket watches, old dishes, and other knick-knacks, but not the context that brings those inanimate objects to life. Sadly, volumes and volumes of human treasure have been lost forever.

We believe the key to building our own legacy and preserving the legacies of others is to find ways of creating and capturing those fleeting moments when ordinary yet extraordinarily amazing women and men open up their hearts and pour out the magical pixie dust of life: the thousands and millions of remembered moments that together make each one of us a unique and precious human being. When our stories continue to be told, we're really still alive. When the bits and pieces of our lives continue to speak in the stories we've told, the library remains open, and we bless others—including generations yet unborn—with the true wealth of a lifetime.

In our view, the first step on this long and critical journey of saving this human wealth is to develop an understanding of the incomparable role of story in the human experience. We believe that in millions of ways large and small, stories matter. ∞

CHAPTER 2

STORIES MATTER

"TO BE A PERSON IS TO
HAVE A STORY TO TELL."
— ISAK DINESEN

We believe story is our native language. Until we were a dozen or so years old, stories were how we looked at and made sense of the world. It is how our parents taught us right from wrong. It is how we played (cops and robbers, cowboys and Indians, Barbie and Ken) and how we learned. It is also how we connected and communicated with those around us. It wasn't until later that we learned to be analytical, and even much later that much of our native expression in story was replaced. But a part of us still longs for story, this most human of media.

Scott has had some interesting experiences that helped him appreciate the importance of communicating in our "common native language:" He shares this story.

One of my college degrees is in Portuguese, which I earned after I had spent a number of years in Brazil speaking Portuguese most of the time. Unfortunately, I subsequently lived for 20 years in places where no other person spoke Portuguese; consequently I lost the ability to speak comfortably in this second language.

Now I live in the Orlando area and have frequent opportunities to speak Portuguese. But because of that 20-year hiatus, I have to work hard to be fully present in the conversation. I notice how tense I become as I struggle to remember how to express a certain thought or conjugate a particular verb, or construct agreement between nouns and adjectives. I'm sure that I often miss the meanings of the other person's statements, and certainly the nuances of tone and expression.

Occasionally the person I'm speaking with, recognizing that their English is better than my Portuguese, switches the conversation to English. It's amazing for me to notice how I immediately relax, begin to enjoy the exchange of ideas, and grasp the whole conversation.

Similarly, I've discovered in meetings with clients in professional settings that if I change from typical "lawyer-ese" or "financial planner-ese" into the client's native language of story, the whole tone of the conversation changes. They relax, they enjoy the exchange of ideas, and they grasp more of what I'm seeking to share with them. More importantly, they begin to share who they are with me.

Creating stories is the way our brains cope with an unmanageable supply of information. Our brains cannot take in the full range of sensory, mental, and emotional experiences that flood in to them without some sort of artificial frame of reference. In order to cope with the overload, our brains collapse these sensory, mental, and emotional experiences into story. The core of the human mind is a storyteller.

Because we can assemble vast amounts of information in our brains as stories, we are able to retain them, organize them, apply them, and manipulate them. This allows us to function more effectively in the world. Over time, these stories become the reality we live in, much as water is the medium fish swim in. Our lives become not what has happened to us, but the stories we tell about what has happened to us.

This is evidenced by listening to two people who have survived a common traumatic episode. One of them may say, "Oh, what a terrible experience! My life will never be the same. It has ruined everything." The other, having experienced the very same event, may say, "Yes, it was terrible, but just look how blessed I am to have come out of it alive and how much I learned in the process."

Scott observed this phenomenon firsthand when he went to Biloxi, Mississippi, three weeks after Hurricane Katrina. He shares this story:

I was one of several hundred men from our church who rode charter buses all night from Orlando to Biloxi to help clean up the devastation following Hurricane Katrina. Our group was sent to a poor area in East Biloxi about a mile from the ocean. In this area, the modest houses were still standing, but the water had flooded into them up to their attics. Everything inside that was not destroyed by the storm surge was ruined by the heat and humidity, because they had been barricaded off and closed up during the three weeks since the hurricane.

Because I have no particularly useful manual skills, I was assigned to one of the so-called "muck-out crews." Our job was to carry everything from the flooded houses and pile the whole moldy mess in giant mounds near the street where it could be hauled away. Then we would rip out the water-logged cabinets and the soggy sheet rock, exposing the studs with the hope that eventually they would dry out and the owners could rebuild.

It was heart-breaking to see people who had so little to start with, who had lost literally everything they owned in the world. Many we met in the neighborhood were understandably depressed, dejected, and angry because of their suffering and misfortune.

One of the families we helped was an older black couple. Their house was a bit larger than others in the area, but they too had lost everything. Although their experience during the storm and in the aftermath was equally as harrowing and tragic as their neighbors, their attitudes were completely different.

As we worked to put all their ruined possessions on the street, the husband opened up and told me what had happened. He said they had built their house a year or so after Hurricane Camille devastated the Mississippi Gulf Coast in 1969. They had designed their house to stand at least a foot higher than the high water mark for Camille, and thus they assumed they would be safe at home when Katrina hit. Unfortunately, the water quickly rose past the high water mark for Camille and began to flood their house. When the water was waist deep in the house, they decided they'd better get out.

Neither one of the couple could swim, but their adult daughter who was with them was a strong swimmer. She went outside in the thick of the storm and, as luck would have it, found a boat being blown down the street. She was able to retrieve it and bring it back to the porch. She helped her parents and their dog get into the boat. They then set off for a relative's two-story house a few blocks away. The winds and rain were fierce, and it was difficult for them to control the boat. They saw a woman they recognized clinging to a lamppost, but they were unable to get to her. They never saw her again.

With hard work and fervent prayer, they managed to make it to their relative's house. By the time they got there, the water was already above the windows of the first floor. Their daughter jumped out of the boat, broke out one of the first floor windows, swam up inside the house, and found the stairwell. She went to a second floor window, and pulled her parents in through that window. They rode out the storm in the second floor of the relative's house.

Leaving their house turned out to be a smart decision because the water ended up rising above the level of the ceiling. In a nearby house, a large family tried to stay in their house by wearing life jackets. Unfortunately, when the water rose past the level of the ceiling, they were pinned between the water and the ceiling and all were drowned.

Like everyone in the neighborhood, this courageous family lost everything they owned. Our crew of two dozen men spent more than a day hauling their possessions and piling them on the street and then stripping out the waterlogged sheet rock. But unlike their neighbors, who were bitter and miserable, they were thankful for our help and intensely grateful for what they saw as God's grace in helping them survive the storm. They said, "Yes we did lose everything, but we still have our lives. That's what matters most of all. God spared us and we can start again."

A shared event; common experiences; but very different stories.

Added together, these story-experiences constitute the themes of our lives. Over time, who we are becomes inseparable from the stories we tell about who we are. "'Who are you?' someone asks. 'I am the story of myself,' comes the answer." (M. Scott Momaday) The acclaimed Nigerian novelist, Chinua Achebe, has written: "We create stories and stories then create us. It is a rondo." Clarissa Pinkola Estes expressed much the same sentiment when she said, "The stories have grown the storytellers, grown them into who they are." And thus, in the words of Reynolds Price, "[t]he sound of story is the dominant sound of our life."

There are a number of reasons stories matter; we think three are especially compelling: First, **stories allow us to have a greater impact in the lives of others.** They allow us to teach with greater effectiveness. They carry our ideas and values with more force into the hearts of others.

Second, **stories help us connect with others.** They help us see ourselves as members of a community of fellow human travelers and make us mindful that we are not alone in our journey.

And finally, **stories help us find meaning and control in our lives.** They help us make sense of the world and of our lives as we continue our journey. They empower us to choose not only where we will go on our journey but also where we have been and what impact those travels will have on us.

Stories allow us to have a greater impact in the lives of others.

"TELL ME A FACT AND I'LL LEARN.
TELL ME A TRUTH AND I'LL BELIEVE.
TELL ME A STORY AND IT
WILL LIVE IN MY HEART FOREVER.
—STEVE SABO

Stephen Denning begins *The Leader's Guide to Storytelling,* his ground-breaking book about the application of story in the business environment, with this sentence: "This book is an account of a simple but powerful idea: the best way to communicate with the people you are trying to lead is very often through a story." Our message is similar. **The best way to communicate with the people you love, the people with whom you want to share the most important learning and insights and feelings of your life, is very often through a story.**

Darlynn Morgan of Newport Beach, California, knows first-hand the impact a story can have in a person's life. She shares this story:

One of the most meaningful gifts anyone ever gave me was the journal my husband Jack kept during the months we were engaged. In it he wrote his thoughts and feelings about our relationship, the things we had gone through together in getting to that point in our lives, and what was in his heart as we were preparing to be married.

The night before our wedding, Jack surprised me with it as a wedding gift. I had no idea he was keeping a journal. Wow, it meant so much to me! What an amazing testament of his love for me. What a wonderful way for us to begin our life together.

We were deeply in love and the first years of our marriage were filled with joy and happiness. But then, much sooner than we ever expected, some very dark days came to us. About two and a half years after we were married, Jack came home from work with bad stomach cramps. We went to the emergency room where they took x-rays and made a number of tests, but they couldn't figure out what was wrong with him. They checked him into the hospital, made some more tests, and took CAT scans.

I'll never forget the look on the doctor's face when he came in to give us the results: it was cancer and it was bad. It was an aggressive form that had already metastasized and spread. It was killing Jack. Even though he was only 36 years old, he had only months to live.

A lot happens inside you when you're thrown into a situation like that. Jack and I had time to think about his legacy and the meaning of life, but it just wasn't the best time for that. When you're in crisis mode and dealing with the pain and the treatments and everything, you don't think very clearly. It's just too sad. In 2001, just 14 months after the diagnosis, Jack died.

I was left in the middle of a huge life transition. It was a difficult struggle to make sense of life. In those dark days of grief, I turned to Jack's journal, and it was like water for my soul. That journal told the story of our young love during the good days, the happy days. I desperately needed that, because we both had some very hard days as he was going through cancer, days when I didn't always feel loved or appreciated. It was soothing and reassuring to read his words and remember those times when we were young and so much in love.

Jack's journal and the stories he recorded there were a priceless treasure to me and forever will be. Jack showed me that a legacy project, any legacy project, is really a gift for the people we love the most. I'm so grateful that Jack thought enough of me and loved me enough to write the journal for me. Even though Jack died and I will someday die too, our love will never die. Jack's journal is evidence of that.

Darlynn's story demonstrates what we and Stephen Denning are trying to convey: there's something very different about the way a story touches us and inspires us and moves us to action, compared to other ways of communicating.

It is not altogether clear why this is so, but we believe it has to do with the way the two sides of our brains operate. The left hemisphere is the critical, analytical side. Its function is to process numbers, evaluate data, and keep things neat and tidy. The right hemisphere, by contrast, is the intuitive, creative side. Its function is to think imaginatively, handle abstractions, and form and decipher stories. Storytelling and story listening are right-brain activities.

We picture that when story-based information is directed toward our brains, it gets routed to the right side, whereas numbers, statistics, and logical arguments are steered to the left side. Upon arrival, bundles of information sent to the left side (numbers, statistics, and logical arguments) are scrutinized and critiqued carefully and skeptically, because that's what the left brain does. Story-based information, on the other hand, is subject to less cynical review because that's the way the right brain operates. It's as if stories bypass the harsher scrub-down and go straight into the system. And since most of our important decisions are made intuitively and then later justified analytically, stories can be very potent in moving us to action. When it comes to touching hearts and affecting behavior, a well-placed story is almost always more effective than numbers, statistics, and logical arguments.

Stories help us connect with others.

"IT IS BY LEARNING TO LISTEN
TO ONE ANOTHER AND BY SHARING
OUR STORIES THAT WE DISCOVER
OUR SHARED HUMANITY."
—JAMES ROOSE-EVANS

We have learned that the real ties that bind, regardless of the type of relationship, are stories. Sharing stories is an honoring, intimate experience that results in feelings of closeness and affection.

This is true whether the people involved have known each other for decades or have never met. We've seen how old friends can meet after years of absence, and with the telling of only a few tales of what they've each been doing in all that time, it's as if they were never apart. Stories re-ignite connections long dormant.

They can also fire up new relationships almost immediately. For example, Scott's company, SunBridge, offers a unique two-day professional training program called the Legacy Builder Retreat. On dozens of occasions during the past five years, this Retreat has brought together a roomful of total strangers (in many cases hardened professionals like attorneys, financial planners, funeral directors, and accountants) in a sterile hotel meeting room, mixed them together randomly, and thrown them headlong into story-sharing activities. The result: at the end of one day, complete strangers have become great friends. At the end of two days, the whole group is making plans to stay in touch, exchanging addresses and phone numbers, and promising to keep each other informed about matters in their professional and personal lives. The secret: we human beings give our hearts to those who listen to our stories, and we cherish those whose stories we have truly heard, for now we understand their world.

Peggy participated in the Legacy Builder Retreat and has this to say about her experience there:

I'd already known and been affiliated with Scott and Sunbridge for a number of years before attending the Legacy Builder Retreat. I had made new friends, discovered new ways to improve the quality of my law practice with my partner, Randy Bryan, including team building, goal setting, practice management and becoming a Level Three Advisor. On the eve of the retreat, Scott hosted a small get-to-know-you reception. As expected, I knew most everyone present. Little did I know that my relationship with one of the participants was about to change forever.

For one of the exercises called "Your Life in a Brown Paper Bag," we were asked to bring a couple of items that had special meaning to us and then to tell each other in a small group the story about each of the items we had chosen. One of the members of our group was a man I'd known for a while but we didn't have a close connection. The stories about the items he brought intrigued me and caught my attention. I wanted to know more.

As a result, when it came time for "Priceless Conversations," this man and I chose to work together. This was the part of the program where we shared stories about our lives, about our families and our definition of success. I was nervous but also anxious to both tell my story and to hear his.

It was his turn to share and mine to listen and give perfect attention. He began, slowly, hesitantly, to share the story of his adult life. He shared the details of meeting and marrying his wife, of having two children, and then surviving divorce. He talked about the hope of finding new love and a new life. He told me about his business, his struggles and his successes.

When we were finished, our relationship was transformed. No longer could we be strangers passing through this world without a connection. We were now permanently bonded through the power of our stories, through the honest sharing of heartfelt feelings, without fear of judgment or recrimination.

Today, whenever I encounter him, it's with the greatest of affection. I remember saying in my appreciation of him at the end of the program that since I'd never had a brother, I would be proud to consider him as my older brother, as part of my family—someone to look up to and to cherish. I value his friendship to this day—all as a result of sharing his stories.

In addition to building and growing friendships, story sharing helps us learn from others. Through others' stories we gain strength, overcome adversity, and are inspired to reach for the stars. We also develop empathy. "For the duration of a story, children may sense how it is to be old, and the elderly may recall how it is to be young; men may try on the experiences of women, and women those of men. Through stories, we reach across the rift not only of gender and age but also of race and creed, geography and class, even the rifts between species or between enemies." (Scott Russell Sanders)

In sharing stories, we are briefly able to see the world—or at least a part of it—from another's vantage point. We take in their words and tone through our senses and send them on to our minds, where they become the catalyst for our own internal reconstruction of the life experiences they are sharing with us. Their stories remake the neuron structure of our brains, and thus they literally become a part of us. True empathy and connection occur.

This happens because "we're all storytellers. We all live in a network of stories. There isn't a stronger connection between people than storytelling," (Jimmy Neil Smith) and because "the *sine qua non* of storytelling is human mutuality, human connection." (Robert Coles)

Just as story sharing builds human-to-human connections, conversely, whenever people reduce or terminate story sharing between themselves, their relationships are weakened. If one looks closely at any relationship that is fading or already dead, it can be seen that the parties to the relationship—whether friends, a married couple, family members, management and labor, or even nations—no longer share stories. In fact, if one works back upstream to the point in time when the relationship turned from good to bad, it will become apparent that it was in that moment that the parties stopped listening to each other's stories and stopped trying to share them with each other. We're not sure which is cause and which is effect, but we are certain that, left unchecked, the cessation of story sharing is an unmistakable harbinger of the demise of the relationship. Strong and lasting human relationships require the sharing of stories.

Stories help us find meaning and control in our lives.

"THE STORIES THAT PEOPLE TELL
ARE THE CONTAINER THAT
HOLDS THEIR WORLD TOGETHER
AND GIVES MEANING TO THEIR LIVES."
ANDREW RAYMER

Every event in life is subject to dozens if not hundreds of different interpretations. Multiply the millions of events that make up even a year in our lives, and we start to see that the possible combinations of interpretations are infinite. How then are we to make sense of the world around us?

It is our view that we do so by turning those millions of events into stories, then we live our lives according to the stories we have created around those events. In the words of the French author Jean-Paul Sartre: "A man is always a teller of tales, he lives surrounded by his stories and the stories of others, he sees everything that happens to him through them, and he tries to live his own life as if he were telling a story." Similarly, Canadian Dan Yashinsky wrote: "The tales we cherish are tools for making sense of our journey."

Stories serve as a buffer, so to speak, between the raw, unfiltered reality of the world and the life we each live. This is actually good news for each of us, because it means that we can improve virtually anything about our lives by re-formulating and re-telling the stories we tell around that thing. "In the degree that we remember and retell our stories and create new ones, we become the authors, the authorities, of our own lives." (Sam Keen) This gives us the freedom to shape our personal world.

"The real difference between telling what happened and telling a story about what happened is that instead of being a victim of our past, we become a master of it. We can't change our past, but we can change where we stand when we look at it." (Donald Davis)

The power of story allows us to select the life we choose to live. "Engaging in personal storytelling can be one of the most comprehensive, healing, and useful ways of validating experiences that we tend to reject. Through transforming our negative, painful, or chaotic experiences into stories, we take responsibility for them, and we bring them to bear more constructively on our lives." (Jack Maguire)

If we fail to exercise this phenomenal human capacity, we may become stuck in a bleak and oppressive prison of our own making. "Those who do not have power over the story that dominates their lives, power to retell it, rethink it, deconstructed, joke about it, and change it as times change, truly are powerless, because they cannot think new thoughts." (Salman Rushdie)

Richard Stone expertly describes this aspect of story and gives an example in his book *The Healing Art of Storytelling*, in a section called "Becoming Your Own Author":

> To transform your pain, you must become the author of your own story. Assuming authorship gives you complete literary license to do whatever you choose. It's your life and your story. As author, you are father and mother to yourself. Stories that enslave you in the here and now can be re-crafted to empower a different outcome. And, like a nurturing parent, you can gently select new aspects of your story to emphasize, freeing you to experience new feelings and possibilities.

A powerful way to transform your tales is to play with their modality. We now know that humor is a physical and emotional healing force. When we can laugh at ourselves and the facts of our lives, it will not change what happened, but we will be changed and released from the heavy burden of tragedy and misfortune. Even the most sacrosanct subjects are open to this form of review. For example, when my mother suffered a stroke in 1983, my brother and I assumed the responsibility for arranging the funeral. She had been deteriorating over the last twenty-four hours, and the doctors had told us that once her respirator was detached, she would live for only a few minutes. In the midst of this sad drama, we went to a funeral home to select a casket. Given that Jewish law dictates a wooden casket, our choices were narrowed. The director guided us upstairs, where a sample of each model was handsomely displayed. Until we asked, he didn't mention anything about price. His sales presentation focused strictly on the fine workmanship of each casket. My brother interrupted him. "What's the difference between these two? You say this one is $600 more, but they look exactly the same." With a straight face, the director informed us that the difference was like night and day. While the first casket was a quality product (they would not be offering it otherwise!), the more expensive model would command such a high price because it used dowels made of oak instead of metal. My brother and I looked at each other. We looked at the casket. Then we looked at the somber face of our casket salesman and broke into hysterical laughter.

I think my mother would have appreciated this ludicrous scene. She had a great sense of humor and would have been laughing, too. When I tell about her passing, I choose to focus on this story rather than the unpleasant details of the hospital and the enormous grief we all experienced. Even in dying, she made us laugh, and that's the way I like to remember her.

This ability to tell new stories and think new thoughts about our own lives sets us free to live life to the fullest. Our ability to reframe the stories we have created about other people can have equally dramatic results. Stephen R. Covey shares this story in *The Seven Habits of Highly Effective People*:

I remember . . . one Sunday morning on a subway in New York. People were sitting quietly—some reading newspapers, some lost in thought, some resting with their eyes closed. It was a calm, peaceful scene.

Then suddenly, a man and his children entered the subway car. The children were so loud and rambunctious that instantly the whole climate changed.

The man sat down next to me and closed his eyes, apparently oblivious to the situation. The children were yelling back and forth, throwing things, even grabbing people's papers. It was very disturbing. And yet, the man sitting next to me did nothing.

It was difficult not to feel irritated. I could not believe that he could be so insensitive as to let him his children run wild like that and do nothing about it, taking no responsibility at all. It was easy to see that everyone else on the subway felt irritated, too. So finally, with what I felt was unusual patience and restraint, I turned to him and said, "Sir, your children are really disturbing a lot of people. I wonder if you couldn't control them a little more?"

The man lifted his gaze as if to come to a consciousness of the situation for the first time and said softly, "Oh, you're right. I guess I should do something about it. We just came from the hospital where their mother died about an hour ago. I don't know what to think, and I guess they don't know how to handle it either."

Can you imagine what I felt at that moment? My paradigm shifted. Suddenly I saw things differently, and because I *saw* it differently, I *thought* differently, I *felt* differently, I *behaved* differently. My irritation vanished. I didn't have to worry about controlling my attitude or my behavior; my heart was filled with the man's pain. Feelings of sympathy and compassion flowed freely. "Your wife just died? Oh, I'm so sorry! Can you tell me about it? What can I do to help?" Everything changed in an instant.

Our innate human ability to reframe a situation or a set of events in terms of a different story gives us broad control over how we experience life, both our own and those of others. "Some people think we are made of flesh and blood and bones. Scientists say we're made of atoms. But I think we're made of stories. When we die, that's what people remember, the stories of our lives and the stories that we told." (Ruth Stotter)

The Dangers of "Destorification"

One of the dramatic changes of our modern industrial, technological world is the reduction in opportunities for sharing and saving personal stories. Jack Maguire described this phenomenon in *The Power of Personal Storytelling*:

Once upon a time, when people made more of their own things, they created more stories about their life experiences. They told these tales to each other regularly, gracefully, and productively. They did it to give each other insights, to entertain each other and to engage each other in times of celebration, trial, mourning, or reverence, but primarily they did it to connect with each other. Sharing real-life stories was an essential element in forging friendships, alliances, families, and communities. It brought individuals a greater intimacy with each other and, simultaneously, a stronger sense of self.

Since that time, for all the wonderful progress made in communication technology, social welfare, education, and health care, the world has grown alarmingly less personal. People have given over much of their individual power to the collective, and have let themselves be recently distracted from personal storytelling by flashier but ultimately less gratifying activities that compete for their attention. As a result, we citizens of today's world have each lost some of our core vitality—our feeling of having direct contact with the lives we lead, of relating meaningfully with others, and of being individuals in our own right, with our own clear identities.

We agree that today's frenetic, multitasking, 24/7 culture does not provide much support for the storying process. Our good friend Richard Stone highlighted the dangers associated with this loss and even coined a term to describe this phenomenon in his masterful book, *The Healing Art of Storytelling*. He writes:

Just as clear-cutting an old growth forest leads to a phenomenon called deforestation—the stripping of the landscape of more than just trees—our culture has been devastated by the loss of storytelling as a tool for communicating, passing on values, learning, and, most importantly, healing. I call it *destorification*. Its effect is as devastating as its ecological cousin's. When you cut down the trees you also destroy the multitude of microenvironments in which a host of other living creatures make their homes. Without the rich variety of trees, life cannot be sustained. Sadly, replanting as we practice it in this country does not recreate a forest. Row after row of tall pines do not entice the rich web of life to return. So it is with destorification. When social and economic pressures led to the disintegration of the intergenerational family, and, more recently, the breakdown of the nuclear family, something much deeper than a way of life died.

Despite the pressures of our current culture, we remain optimistic about the ongoing role of story in the future. Notwithstanding a less-than-supportive environment, we believe story will continue to play a significant role in our lives, primarily because the creation and sharing of stories is such an engrained part of who we are as human beings. Jack Maguire seems to share our positive outlook.

Like our ancestors, we are each personal storytellers to some degree whether or not we think of ourselves that way. Telling personal tales is an intrinsic part of being human. On a daily basis, as we interact with others, we inevitably wind up talking about our past or present experiences. Some of us carry this first-person narrative beyond our own homes and the places where we visit, work, and play, into classrooms, boardrooms, chat rooms, pulpits, therapy sessions, talk shows, rap concerts, or storytelling festivals. (*The Personal Power of Storytelling*)

Ellin Greene and George Shannon said it this way: "Storytelling has been called the oldest and the newest of arts. Human beings seem to have an inbuilt need to structure their world and to communicate their feelings and experiences through storying." Whether we like it or not, or whether we are mindful of it or not, "[m]an is a storytelling animal par excellence. We live for, and die for, our stories." (George Gerbner) It's simply who we are and what we do.

"We all are made of stories. They are as fundamental to our soul, intellect, imagination, and way of life as flesh, bone, and blood to our bodies." (Jack Maguire) ∞

CHAPTER 3

YOUR STORIES MATTER

"WHAT A WONDERFUL LIFE I'VE HAD! I ONLY
WISH I'D REALIZED IT SOONER."
— COLLETTE

We believe there are no "ordinary" people and there are no "ordinary" lives. Each of us is the keeper of an amazing collection of lifetime experiences. And yet, many people, if not most, think of themselves and their lives as quite ordinary. How can this be? We think it's because most people have never turned their jumbled pile of lifetime experiences into stories, and thus, like digging up a pile of uncut, unpolished diamonds that look like dirty old rocks, they cannot appreciate the richness they hold in their own hands. They are living an "unstoried life." "Relatively little of our lives is ever storied. Most of our experiences and perceptions flow into the amorphous black hole that we call our past, never to be recalled, reflected on, or evaluated." (Richard Stone)

Living an "unstoried life" is like walking into a disgustingly cluttered house. All we see around us are piles of junk. We can't find anything and we don't have a clue as to what's under all those stacks. There's nowhere to sit, and there's no way we could ever relax or reflect. Everything is ugly, even though the house underneath it all may be strikingly beautiful. The mess is totally overwhelming because we can't see where to begin to make order of the chaos. And it's unhealthy, dangerously unhealthy, to stay there, both physically and mentally.

We believe there is something wondrous and almost magical for us when we turn our own raw, unrefined life experience into stories. The process of "story-ing" our lives gives us insight, heals us, and connects us more fully with others. "Storytelling is the essential creative force that gives us not just an existence but a life," according to author and storytelling expert Jack Maguire. Sam Keen echoes that thought in *Your Mythic Journey*:

> I can't promise you that your stories will give you certainty or objective truth any more than the ancient myths gave the Hebrews or Greeks accurate maps of the world. They will, however, fill you with the stuff from which romance, tragedy, and comedy are made. They will hollow you out so you can listen to the stories of others, as common and unique as your own. And that remains the best way we storytelling animals have found to overcome our loneliness, develop compassion, and create community.

Jan Gammill of Fruita, Colorado has found great blessings through the process of story-ing her life along with her husband Steve. She shares this story:

> My husband Steve and I have been richly blessed since we started attending and embracing Legacy Building opportunities. Steve has been an attorney for 44 years and has devoted the past 12 years to estate planning. His desire to be the best estate planning attorney he could be and my desire to work more closely with him led us to create our own "Legacy by Stories" program.
>
> We have loved hearing the stories of our clients and learning from their experiences and the threads of wisdom woven through them. However, the greatest blessing I have received has been to learn how to better share stories with my husband about our own lives. Through stories, I've discovered so much about myself and so much about him. I've found that through our shared stories, we've fallen in love all over again, but this time in a much deeper way.

We both entered our marriage with baggage from divorces and mistakes in our earlier years. We both had made a personal commitment to Jesus Christ as our Lord and Savior and thus we knew the slate had been wiped clean. Then from Legacy Building we discovered that we could learn from our past by sharing our stories. We started sharing significant events of our lives and telling about important keepsakes. We pored through photo albums together and shared the experiences captured in the pictures. Through all of this, we listened to each other with our hearts and honored the bravery of the other as we shared stories of some of our difficult times.

One of the things I've come to love is sharing positive stories about our ex-in-laws. Steve told me how his father-in-law was a great role model for him as a young man. He and Steve worked together on construction sites and from that experience Steve learned to appreciate the feeling of success that comes when hard physical labor leads to the completion of a tough job, like building a house. This wonderful man also taught Steve the importance of setting aside time to play after that hard work.

I had the privilege of meeting him and his entire family and playing one of their favorite card games, "Blitz," over a memorable Christmas vacation. What joy to be able to sit around that table and hear story after story that Steve's granddaughters will always treasure! From this whole experience, I learned that if we're able to get our own insecurities out of the way, wonderful memories can be shared and created.

When it was my turn to tell a story about my ex-in-laws, I told Steve how my father-in-law would go for long walks with me in his orchard and talk about education. He had served on a local school board and I was an elementary teacher. He was so wise about how to create a wonderful learning environment for children and I'd soak up his advice. I remember the time he visited my classroom and I said I was thinking about arranging the desks differently, but the custodian was discouraging me because it would be more difficult to clean the floor. Larry laughed and said, "And who's creating this learning environment for the children?"

Because Steve heard these stories and honored my love of this man, we spent a very special time together to introduce him to his great grandsons. During this visit, we were able to record some of his school board experiences, his World War II stories, and his wisdom for his children, his grandchildren, and his great grandsons!

It has been an amazing journey together. We know that we keep these stories in a safe and sacred place. This place is where we go to say, "These are the stories that make us who we are today." Without those stories and the ability to honor them, we would not be able to celebrate where we are today, nor would we be able to pass on to others what we have learned. Sharing our stories has brought us closer as a couple and given us the means to pass on this blessing to our families!

As Jan's story demonstrates, we believe there are several compelling reasons for each of us to turn the raw data of our life experience into story. "Story-ing" our lives gives us insight. It helps us understand what our lives have been—and can be—all about. It helps heal us, allowing us to reach or return to a place of wholeness. It helps us better understand others and empathize with those around us.

In his ground-breaking book, *How to Say it to Seniors,* David Solie writes about what he calls "the mandate of life review." He argues that seniors have a developmental need to reflect on their life and to search within it for their legacy—the impact their life will have on the lives of those around them. He states:

[I]n order to go forward to accept our lives and prepare for a peaceful death, we must look backward and recontextualize the events we've lived. If we go forward without looking back, the journey is extremely unsatisfactory.

Life review isn't about the need to erect a monument in our honor. It is about reviewing what happened in our life and assigning new or different meanings to events, then considering how those recontextualized events figure into the way we want to be remembered.

We believe the process he describes as "recontextualization" is essentially what we call "story-ing" our lives. We also believe it's not just for seniors. While it may become a developmental imperative when the reality of our own mortality starts to bear down on us, it is equally valuable regardless of our age or station in life.

When we turn raw experience into story, we discover an orderliness and a flow about our lives. We begin to recognize the patterns and themes. "Stories become the vehicle by which we organize the things that happen to us. It's also our way of telling time. Our life's story takes shape like chapters in a book, each in its proper place, one following the next, explaining why things were as they were, lending logic to our decisions and bringing meaning to what might otherwise be a collection of unrelated events. Without stories, life becomes a book cover without the pages—nice to look at, but not very fulfilling." (Richard Stone)

As we continue to "story" our lives, we discover, sometimes to our great surprise, that we have accomplished much and overcome significant obstacles. We uncovered hidden treasures of wisdom.

In a process we call "Priceless Conversations," we ask our clients questions that help them remember bits and pieces of their lives in the form of stories. We record their answers for others to hear later. After each Priceless Conversation is recorded, we invite the clients to listen to the interviews themselves and report back to us what they thought as they heard themselves. Almost without exception, they report surprise at the important insights and life-lessons they had within themselves.

The story-ing process brings to the surface facets of our lives that have lain dormant or that we have long forgotten. "Although setbacks of all kinds may discourage us, the grand, old process of storytelling puts us in touch with strengths we may have forgotten, and wisdom that has faded or disappeared, and with hopes that have fallen into darkness." (Nancy Mellon)

On some occasions the story-ing process allows us to drill down to hidden pockets of profound understanding. Story-ing seems to be an antidote to the shallowness of modern life. James P. Carroll, writing in the October 2002 issue of *O Magazine*, ably describes how this happens:

We spend most of our time and energy in a kind of horizontal thinking. We move along the surface of things going from one quick base to another, often with a frenzy that wears us out. We collect data, things, people, ideas, "profound experiences," never penetrating any of them. But there are other times. There are times when we stop. We sit still. We lose ourselves in a pile of leaves or its memory. We listened and breezes from a whole other world began to whisper. Then we began our "going down."

Often, in the familiar or even mundane parts of our lives, we find exciting new vistas and panoramas by looking anew at our lives through story. It's true, we believe, as Marcel Proust wrote, that "[t]he real voyage of discovery lies not in seeing new landscapes but in having new eyes." New stories give us new eyes for the world, including the "ordinary" parts of the world we call our own lives. We have learned in the course of helping hundreds of people tell their stories that all of us can discover important insights about life.

One of those important insights, as Jan Gammill noted, is that the story-ing process can lead to personal healing. Old hurts and long-ago injuries can be cleaned out and re-bandaged, lanced and drained, even surgically removed, by re-visiting them and creating or revising our stories about them. "Stories heal because we become whole again through them. In the process of discovering our story, we restore those parts of ourselves that have been scattered, hidden, suppressed, denied, distorted, forbidden." (Deena Metzger) Because we have the power to decide which stories we will jettison and which ones we will hold and tell and then live by regarding any segment of our life, we hold the remedy for many of life's ills in our own hands.

We occasionally hear people say they can't share their stories because they are too painful. Undoubtedly many are. Without in any way minimizing the brutality, deprivation, or injustice many people have endured in their lives, we extend a kind and gentle invitation to those who feel that way to give voice to their story so their healing can begin. They can find an empathic listener who can offer full and non-judgmental attention, and put the events surrounding their injury into a narrative. We have learned that "a story is a way to say something that can't be said in any other way," (Flannery O'Connor) and that "all sorrows can be borne if you put them in story or tell a story about them." (Isak Dinesen) "This is a yearning we all share to some degree. Each one of us, both within our own families and communities, as well as among those of different faiths, traditions, and even ancient enmities, needs urgently to be heard if healing is to be found." (James Roose-Evans)

Because story-ing our lives helps us better understand ourselves, it helps us better connect with others. "When one is a stranger to oneself then one is estranged from others too. If one is out of touch with oneself, then one cannot touch others." (Ann Morrow Lindberg) Once we are able, through our stories, to celebrate our own uniqueness as a human being, we can more fully appreciate and even celebrate the uniqueness of those around us.

We've found that people use lots of different excuses to keep themselves from enjoying this magnificent opportunity of story-ing their life. Among the most common we hear are these: "I don't have a very interesting life;" "I can't remember any stories;" or "I'm just too busy."

"I don't have a very interesting life."

This line of excuses comes in a thousand different flavors: "I'm too old." "I'm too young." "I'm one of a million from this city, same as all the rest." "I grew up in the suburbs—what could I possible say about that." "I'm just an ol' country boy and nothin' ever happens around here." "I have the most boring job in the world." "I was pretty much invisible in high school, and things haven't changed a bit since then." "Got married, had kids, stayed home, kids are growing up too fast—what's to tell?" "Got married, had kids, stayed home, husband left me, back at work, single mom—what's to tell?" "Never got married, worked all my life, same dull job—what's to tell?"

There is a compelling bit of irony here: the reason we think we have nothing interesting in our lives to story is because we haven't tried to story our lives. Turning the raw material of our life experience into stories is what creates an interesting life. Jack Maguire in *The Power of Personal Storytelling* explains this curious phenomenon:

> Getting involved in developing and telling stories keeps us from unfairly dismissing large portions of our lives as boring, routine, or unremarkable. It's a common type of self-denial that I sometimes commit...and one that I hear repeatedly in my storytelling workshops. Personal storytelling helps us go beyond these tired, easy, blind responses and see the full range of wondrous moments and meaningful themes that exist in our day-to-day lives. We revitalize our sense of the miraculous. Viewed with this kind of

sensitivity, even the most apparently featureless, unexplored life can metamorphose into a story-rich odyssey.

One of the magical features of stories is that they can be triggered quickly, simply, and easily. One of America's great storytellers, Jimmy Neil Smith, has said, "Whatever their nature, stories began, and have always begun, quite simply: with a moment, an experience, a feeling." Henry Miller described that fairy-tale moment as follows: "The moment one gives close attention to anything, even a blade of grass, it becomes a mysterious, awesome, indescribably magnificent world in itself."

An old story about a 19th Century scullery maid in England illustrates how focusing on a small object or a brief moment of our lives can be the catalyst for discovering intensely interesting stories. On her day off, she attended a lecture by a famous professor. He asserted that each person is surrounded by an interesting world and is capable of living an interesting life.

The maid, considering her wretched working and living conditions and lack of any apparent opportunity to change her lot in life, approached the professor to argue that his theory didn't apply to her.

He answered her with a question. "What do you do all day?" he asked.

"I sit on the back stoop and peel potatoes for my master's kitchen," she replied.

"And where do your feet rest while you peel potatoes?" queried the professor.

"On bricks," she said.

"Well, then, I'd like you to write me a letter and tell me all you know about bricks," he challenged her.

She stomped off, not pleased with his treatment of her, but his challenge stuck with her. When she could steal away from her work, she read all she could about bricks in her master's library, and when that was exhausted, she went to the university's library. She wrote him a letter of several dozen pages explaining all the different types and uses of bricks, how they are made, their history, and the role they played in the development of architecture.

Within a few weeks, he invited her to his office.

"I found your letter about bricks to be so interesting and so well researched that I edited it and sent it to a trade journal for brick manufacturers," he said. "It was accepted for publication, and here is a check to you for 100 pounds."

Excited about the money but still not convinced, the maid thanked him but fired back, "So I got lucky this once, but that still doesn't prove I have anything but a dull and tedious life."

His quick reply: "What is under the bricks where your feet rest while you peel potatoes for your master's kitchen?"

Her one word response: "Ants."

"Write me all you know about ants."

Several months later, she sent him a thick manuscript on the subject of ants.

In a few short weeks, he wrote her that her manuscript was the most thorough and accurate on the subject that he or any of his colleagues had ever seen, and it was to be published by one of the major scientific publishers in the country.

With the royalties from her book and the lectures she gave, the maid left her job and went to explore all the unusual places in the world inhabited by ants that she had learned about in her research and writing.

Any blade of grass, any brick, any ant, or any remembered moment of our lives may be the catalyst to help us realize that we have untold numbers of interesting stories inside of us. Once we start to create those stories, we find that life takes on excitement and meaning. Thus, we believe there are no dull or uninteresting lives—only lives that are still unstoried. Every person we have ever met has a unique, eye-opening, heart-pounding, gut-wrenching set of stories inside of them. All they need is a listening, appreciative ear and a word or two of encouragement.

"I can't remember any stories."

This excuse is similar to the one about not having an interesting life. In this case, story*telling* begets story *memories*. We will discover memories to spin into stories as we begin to tell stories. "I used to think I didn't have many personal stories to tell because I didn't have many clear memories. Now I know it was the other way around: I didn't have many clear memories because I didn't tell many personal stories." (Jack Maguire) Once we start creating stories, we find that story-worthy memories start pouring back to us.

Story-worthy memories can be coaxed out of us sometimes with the use of story-leading questions and also with the help of certain trigger words. For example, here is a list developed by our friend Richard Stone. We find that asking people to remember a situation involving one or two of these things, where they were, who they were with, and what happened to them almost always results in a story.

Adventure	Flood	Reading
Ball game	Flying	Relative
Beach	Gift	Sailing
Bicycle	Girlfriend	School
Birthday	Haircut	Sister
Boyfriend	Hero	Snowstorm
Broken	Hiding place	Spring
Brother	Holiday meal	Success
Burnt food	Hurricane	Summer
Business	Job	Swimming
Camp	Lie	Teacher
Car accident	Locked out	Travel
Country	Lost	Tree
Dancing	Math	Trouble
Doctor	Mountain	Vacation
Explosion	Party	War
Failure	Pet	Water
Fall	Picnic	Weeping
Favorite store	Plane crash	Winter
Fire	Political election	
First Impression	Rain	

This is by no means an exhaustive list, and any number of other similar words can be used in the same manner.

Sometimes when people say they can't remember stories, they are really saying they're unsure of certain facts or dates they believe to be essential to the telling of a story and they don't want to tell a story without every fact and detail in place. Our advice in that situation is to go with what you know or believe to be so. Storytelling is like the game of horseshoes: close enough counts. Take the attitude of Jean-Jacques Rousseau when he said, "I may omit or transpose facts, or make mistakes about dates. But I cannot go wrong about what I felt, or about what my feelings have led me to do; and these are the chief subjects of my story." A story with an occasional missing or misstated detail is still far better than a story that is never told at all.

"I'm just too busy."

Being too busy can definitely get in the way of story-ing our lives. Unfortunately, it can create havoc in lots of other ways too. More than 20 years ago, Jeremy Rifkin in *Time Wars* warned of the dangers to the human psyche of too much speed.

> We have quickened the pace of life only to become less patient. We have become more organized, but less spontaneous, less joyful. We are better prepared to act on the future, but less able to enjoy the present and reflect on the past. Humanity has created an artificial time environment punctuated by mechanical contrivances and electronic impulses.

One hundred and fifty years before that, visionaries like Walt Whitman were warning that the industrial revolution (not to mention the digital revolution) was artificially accelerating the tempo of people's lives to the point where humans were losing touch with their inner rhythms and the natural pulse of their thoughts and emotions. Whitman urged us to appreciate and occasionally cultivate idle time as a way to refresh the soul, in order to become more receptive to the human part of us.

Story may be the ideal antidote for too much busy-ness in our lives. Taking the time to tell our stories ironically creates a sense of having more time. Story-ing our lives pulls us briefly out of the rushing current of day-to-day life and back into the natural flow of our inner selves. It allows time for reflection and provides a vantage point for a wider perspective. From that vantage point, we not only see *things* more clearly, we see *ourselves* more clearly. We recognize that "[t]he present is only a moment and the past is one long story. Those who don't tell stories and don't hear stories live only for the moment, and that isn't enough." (I. B. Singer)

So we urge you to put aside your excuses and turn your lifetime of experiences and perceptions into stories. We promise you'll be richly blessed in doing so. One of those blessings, we believe, will be to recognize what a wonderful life you've had! ∽

CHAPTER 4

SHARING YOUR STORIES MATTERS

"THERE IS NO AGONY
LIKE BEARING AN UNTOLD
STORY INSIDE OF YOU."
—MAYA ANGELOU

We believe there is a deep human longing in each of us to share stories, both to tell them and to hear them from others. This seems to come hard-wired inside us, without regard to culture or nurture. "Inside each of us is a natural born storyteller, waiting to be released," said Robin Moore. We yearn to communicate with others the story-ing that is going on constantly within each of us.

Expressing our stories aloud makes our internal story-ing process all the more valuable. Like a beautiful butterfly emerging from a tight cocoon, something changes with the telling of the story that can never happen as long as it stays inside of us. "Telling someone about your experience breeds new life into it, moving it out of the inchoate swirl of unconsciousness into reality. It takes on form, and allows us to examine it from all sides." (Mandy Aftel) In their telling, our stories come alive, and as they do, so do we.

Telling our stories opens a world of emotional connections between us and the listener. "Sharing a story stirs the imagination, pulls a heartstring, tickles the funny bone; it allows us to give the greatest gift—a part of our self." (Joan Branyan Ward and John Ward) Sharing stories helps us combat a sense of being alone in the world, because as we do, we invite others into our world and they invite us to visit theirs.

> Telling a story, especially about ourselves, may be one of the most personal and intimate things we can do. Through storytelling we can come to know who we are in new and unforeseen ways. We can also reveal to others what is deepest in our hearts, in the process building bridges. The very act of sharing a story with another human being contradicts the extreme isolation that characterizes so many of our lives. (Richard Stone, *The Healing Art of Storytelling*)

In a sense, sharing stories is a wonderful pretext for getting together in a personal way. The stories of our lives are rich in learning and nourishment for others, and likewise theirs are for us. We learn so much and grow so much when we share our stories. "In my life, the stories I have heard from my family, my friends, my community, and from willing strangers all over the world have been the true source of my education. They have taught me humor, compassion, and courage." (Holly Near)

Unfortunately, some families raise their children to feel, and some cultures—ours included—teach their members to believe that it's not appropriate to share stories. In such cases, we must make an extra effort to invite the story-sharers all around us (including ourselves) to open up. Fortunately, because of our deep innate desire to share stories, it usually doesn't take much to trigger a cascade of stories. Most of the time, all it takes is for someone to ask the right kind of question and then show a genuine interest in the answer.

In their outstanding book, *Your Client's Story*, Scott West and Mitch Anthony offer an excellent example of both this cultural reticence to share stories and the wonderful discoveries we make when we break through this barrier and start inviting others to share their stories with us.

After presenting a keynote speech (where we always talk about asking people where they are from), Mitch was approached by an advisor who had a story to tell.

"A few months back I was invited to attend a cocktail party at a local old folks' home in Little Rock," he started. "Now I know you're wondering about my social life—and I wondered too as I walked into the event. But it ended up being one of the most fascinating events of my life."

He sat down in a circle of people, all of whom were in their 70s to 90s, and asked the woman next to him, "Where did you grow up?" She told him the exact address. He nearly fell out of his chair. It was the exact address at which he had once lived when he was renting a small house in the back of the property. They had some great laughs and conversation about that old house and the various people that had lived in it through the years.

He then asked her about where she had gone after she moved out of that house. She told him about going to a nearby college where she had roomed with the famous poet, Edna St. Vincent Millay. "How fascinating," the advisor thought, as she described their relationship.

At this point, he began to notice a woman a couple of chairs down who seemed quite tuned in to their conversation. "How about you?" he asked. "Where are you from?"

"Oh me," she replied, "I'm from Wisconsin."

"Really?" he responded. "What did you do in Wisconsin?"

"Oh, I worked for the government," she replied dismissively.

"What did you do with the government?" he inquired further.

"I worked for a United States senator," she said as nonchalantly as possible.

"And which senator was that?" the advisor asked.

"Senator Joseph McCarthy," she informed him. They had a most interesting conversation about those days and what it was like to be on the inside of the most historical period of communist paranoia.

The advisor then noticed a fellow in the circle who had been eavesdropping, so he turned to him and asked, "Well, what's your story?"

"I was just an educator," he said.

"Not just any educator," one of the ladies offered.

"Where were you an educator, and what did you do?" the advisor asked

"I was superintendent of schools right here in Little Rock," he answered.

Then it struck the advisor that there might be another historical figure right there in that small circle. "Were you the school superintendent in 1955?" he queried, referring to the date of the historical civil rights event of the color line being broken at an all-white high school.

"I certainly was," he answered, and they proceeded to have yet another amazing conversation. Needless to say this "geriatric happy hour" turned out to be one of the best parties this advisor had ever wandered into. What are the odds of encountering three such amazing stories in one place in Little Rock? The former roommate of a famous poet, a secretary to a famous and historically significant senator, and a famous figure in the battle for civil rights. Amazing.

What struck that advisor that night was the number of other amazing stories he has failed to hear because he failed to ask and failed to show interest. That's the part that gets to us. How many wonderful, beautiful, interesting, and amazing stories do we walk right by in the average week?

Their question is one we should seriously and repeatedly ask ourselves: **"How many wonderful, beautiful, interesting, and amazing stories do we walk right by in the average week?"** And as a result, what wealth of human treasure do we miss in the process? How golden would our lives be if we only took the time to tap into this rich mother lode from time to time?

We've had the opportunity to share the stories of hundreds of clients over the years, and we can honestly say we've never met an uninteresting person in all that time. In fact, we've become convinced that, as ordinary as they may appear on the surface, there are no ordinary people among us. Every life story we've heard has been absolutely fascinating and it has been a delight to hear them all!

We find we lose our hearts to the people who tell their stories to us. Peggy shares this story about one of those people who came into her life and ended up changing it forever:

Katherine "Kitty" Donaldson and I came to know each other in a typical way—through a business relationship. I was a young broker at a national wire house. As fate would have it, one of the other brokers left for another firm and her accounts were distributed to the other brokers in the office. I ended up with Kitty's account. Dutifully, I called her and the other clients whose accounts I had been assigned to make the appropriate contact and set up a time when we could review their investment history.

And as they say, the rest is history. Kitty was a widow lady in her late 60's, not really old but definitely older than me, at the ripe old age of 24. Her husband had died a few years earlier and they never had any children. We struck up an immediate and unusual friendship—I enjoyed doing things with her and her friends. We enjoyed dog shows, traveling, and happy hour. It was Kitty and her friends who taught me how to drink martinis. My first encounter came one evening when I arrived for an evening chat. The ladies, Kitty and her best friend Margaret, were having a cocktail when I arrived. They inquired as to my preference and I responded, "I'll have whatever you're having." I almost choked! The drink was so strong my eyes watered.

Because of our shared interests and Kitty's warm way of sharing her wisdom through her life stories, she soon became a very special part of my family. She became my mom away from home, giving me advice and providing a support system, and I was like the daughter she never had, providing her with a never-ending dialogue of my life's traumas. I also shared her with my own family back in Maryland. Kitty traveled with me on several occasions from Florida to Maryland to enjoy family holidays.

A few years into our friendship Kitty was diagnosed with liver cancer that had metastasized to other organs. She was ill but made it clear she wasn't going to be a burden on anyone. Despite the fact that she lived in a senior community with levels of care so she could go into a nursing center if necessary, she also made it perfectly clear that this was not her intention. She planned to spend her last days in her home, an independent living cottage.

I wanted a way to remember Kitty that was more than just memories or photographs. One day I set up a video camera while she, Margaret and I were having an informal luncheon in her sunroom. We were talking casually, telling jokes and enjoying each other's company. The stories flowed like water that afternoon. None of our video was scripted or contrived. It was just three friends having fun at lunch. That video is one of my prized possessions. (An interesting side note: when Margaret died, her family sought me out, anxious to get a copy of the video so they could again enjoy seeing their mother and hearing her stories.)

As Kitty's time drew near, she also spent time telling me stories about the possessions she had acquired over a lifetime. I took notes, trying to absorb as much as possible, wanting to capture all of the meaning of her belongings. My attempt fell far short of even adequate. I wish now I had recorded those stories rather than trying to write down what she was saying. Today, more than twenty years later, I can remember very little and I'd have a hard time finding the notebook with all of her instructions. One funny and ironic thing that stands out are two items we failed to discuss. After Kitty died, I discovered two family urns with cremains in her front bedroom. We definitely never discussed what or who these were! Today they remain a loved and valued part of my household as my "guardian angels."

Personal possessions have a unique way of impacting your life. For years, I stored all of Kitty's things in a storage unit—unable to part with any of them—they reminded me of her. Then, little by little, I got them all out, admired them, gave some away and kept some for future enjoyment. I get a great deal of comfort using some of her everyday household items, like an old space heater that still works perfectly today!

I gave one unusual item to my mother-in-law. To me it looked like an ugly glass container. Turns out it's an antique pickle server like one I found in an antique store with a $250 price tag!

More than once I've had a dream in which Kitty returned to earth, alive and well, and looking for all of her things. In horror, I try to explain what I did with them and offer to return everything I still have—and I do have a lot. She picked the right pack rat to care for and love her possessions until the end of my lifetime.

Once we discovered how wonderful it is to hear people's stories, we began to be more inquisitive and intentional about how to draw them out of people. We learned that being an attentive, supportive listener is essential, and we also learned that certain types of questions will spark a good round of stories. As attorneys, we were taught in law school about "leading questions," which guide a witness to testify a certain way. With our discovery that particular questions lead frequently to good stories, it just seemed obvious to us to call them "**story-leading questions.**"

We've found that good story-leading questions exhibit a warm and welcoming interest in the life of another. Good story-leading questions are appropriate to the level of trust and intimacy between those present, and they never put the other person on the spot. Similarly, they never feel judgmental. Good story-leading questions also allow the prospective storyteller a number of ways to answer the question, rather than leaving them only one possible option.

Story-leading questions are like magic matches: they ignite a warm, crackling exchange of life-experiences and life-lessons. Sometimes, they even kindle bonfires of story sharing. A good story-leading question naturally and comfortably invites the other person to recall and share a little bit of their life with the person posing the question.

The number of good story-leading questions is literally infinite, which allows for everyone to develop their own repertoire according to their own style and interest. Here are a few we have found that work well for us, in particular with people we are meeting for the first time, which is usually the most difficult time to get people to share stories.

- Where did you grow up?
- How did you end up here in Central Florida?
- How did the two of you get together? [Then to the other spouse:] Is that the way you remember it?
- How did you get started being a [salesman, teacher, accountant, etc.]?
- Did you always plan to be a [salesman, teacher, accountant, etc.]?
- Tell me a little bit about your grandchildren.
- What do you like about being a grandparent?
- What do you like about this kind of a car?
- That's an interesting [ring, broach, necklace, etc.] you're wearing. What's its history?

We've discovered that as the relationship grows and matures, the wording of story-leading questions becomes less critical. Over time, the level of story sharing will be driven more by the quality of the relationship than the phrasing of the question.

Another key we have found to opening up story sharing is an appropriate balance between telling and listening. It helps if we share a few of our life experiences—sometimes to help "prime the pump," and other times to make sure it doesn't feel like some kind of Spanish inquisition or Dragnet interrogation. On the other hand, it is also vitally important to express lots of interest in others and allow them plenty of time and space to share their narrative. Scott West and Mitch Anthony in *Your Client's Story* have observed an interesting irony in this: we sense the longing in ourselves to tell our story, but we often fail to recognize these same stirrings in those around us:

We all have a biographical impulse that fuels a parade of stories about ourselves, yet we somehow fail to connect the need to tell our own story to the fact that others harbor the same impulse. While every person's story may not be interesting to others, it is interesting to them—and they want to tell it. The problem is that not many people want to sit and hear the story.

The blessing of listening to the legacy stories of a fellow human traveler in the journey of life is a fragile opportunity easily lost. As mentioned previously, seniors have a developmental need to sort through and share their life experiences, and it is easy to miss or discount the importance to them of doing so.

Telling personal stories is a bequest, a deeply meaningful and intimate legacy. Unfortunately, we sometimes fail to recognize these heartfelt gifts and listen with only one ear. When grandma tells us for the fortieth time how she came over to America, we must see this tale as more than just the idle rambling of an old person with a failing memory. She's attempting to keep alive this recollection of her past because without it she is nothing. These are the pages in the book that are hers and hers alone. (Richard Stone, *The Healing Art of Storytelling*)

But the value of listening to another's stories is not limited to seniors; it is a priceless gift to a young child, a struggling teen-ager, a young mother, a middle-age father, an aged widow, or someone of any age. We believe there is nothing more honoring to another human being than to listen with true interest and genuine attention to their stories. This simple act of respect and human kindness can literally change their life. And in the same moment it can change ours as well.

Scott learned this as a teenager. He shares this story:

As far as I was concerned, Arthur Jones was just a mean bully, and I have the scar to prove it.

Shortly after I joined Boy Scouts at age 12, our troop went to a public swimming pool in a nearby town. After swimming, I was getting dressed in a changing stall in the boys' locker room when Arthur pounded on the door and announced that it was "his" stall. I said I was there first and he could have it after I finished dressing.

Accustomed to getting his own way, Arthur was not pleased with my answer. He yanked the door open and proceeded to try to force me out. Even though he was a year and a half older than I and much taller and 40 pounds heavier, I stood my ground. Angry at being challenged, he grabbed me and threw me headlong into the edge of the locker door, causing a two-inch gash in my forehead, just above the hairline. At that point, I ceded possession of the stall.

As much as possible I steered clear of Arthur for the next several years, which wasn't always easy in a place as small as Fruitland. Any unavoidable contact was tense and uncomfortable. In time, Arthur may have grown out of his bully stage but I didn't want to have a thing to do with him.

During the summer when I was 16, I heard about a local farmer who was building a silo and who was paying good money for unskilled laborers. I called around and was lucky enough to get hired. I was told to report for work first thing Monday morning.

I showed up at the appointed hour eager to go to work and then I saw him. It was my old nemesis, Arthur Jones. He had been hired a week earlier, so not only was he my co-worker, in his mind he was my superior. I really needed the money to buy school clothes, so there I was, stuck working with him. Cursing my bad luck, I thought, "I'll just try to stay out of his way and make the best of it." Things were awkward for the next several days as I tried to work around him without really talking to him.

Then one day I was sitting on the shady side of the partially finished silo eating my lunch when Arthur came by and sat down next to me. I groaned inside, but thought it best not to get up and move. He wanted to talk. He wanted to tell me about his trip earlier that summer to a Boy Scout aquatic camp at Conchas Lake in eastern New Mexico. He went there by himself and didn't know a soul, so it was a real struggle trying to fit in. He had to work hard to stay up with some of the others because he hadn't had as many opportunities to swim as they had. It was a challenge to complete the mile swim, but by the end of his week there, he was able to do it. He felt really successful about that. I had always wanted to go to Conchas Lake, so I was very interested in his experience. I found myself listening, in spite of myself. I started asking him questions, wanting to know more about the mile swim and other activities. The more I asked, the more of his story he told.

Something magical happened for me as I listened. Before, he was just a bully to me, and I could dismiss him on that basis. But listening to his experiences, sharing a little slice of his life through his story, changed the way I saw him. It permitted me to allow him to step outside the frame in which I had stuck him (not without cause) and recognize the change and maturity that had happened in his life. Hearing Arthur's story made him more human to me. I could see that humans can make mistakes, and they can also grow out of those old behavior patterns.

My listening and his sharing his story seemed to change him too. He brought up the incident back in the locker room, and said he was sorry it had ever happened, but didn't know what to say to me. He knew he was wrong, he said, but he didn't think I would even let him utter an apology. He said he felt relieved that he was able to tell me he felt bad for hurting me.

Arthur and I worked together on that silo for several more weeks and we became great friends. He started giving me rides to and from work, and we found we had a lot of things in common. Our friendship continued when we went back to school that fall. We were both different people after that. I missed him a lot when he went off to college.

As this narrative illustrates, listening to stories changes the listener and it changes the teller. We kindle a glowing fire of connection, understanding, and learning when we share stories. "We are all wedded to our stories. It doesn't mean we are each hermetically sealed in our own little worlds, impervious to the influence of others. It does mean that the only way to avoid such isolation is to listen, compassionately, to the stories of others." (Daniel Taylor)

We have discovered in our own lives that we are drawn to good story listeners. They are like the pied piper to us—we want to be around them and we'll follow them almost anywhere. We like how it makes us feel when we are listened to. "Listening is a magnetic and strange thing, a creative force. The friends who listen to us are the ones we move toward, and we want to sit in their radius. When we are listened to, it creates us, makes us unfold and expand." (Karl Menninger)

One of the best listeners we know is our dear friend Nancy Kline. Nancy has taught us how to move beyond mere listening to a state of fascinated attention. In her masterful book, *Time to Think,* Nancy describes how real attention is catalytic and ignites the human mind, and compares that to how most people typically "listen" to each other.

Attention, the act of listening with palpable respect and fascination, is the key to a Thinking Environment. Listening of this calibre is enzymatic. When you are listening to someone, much of the quality of what you are hearing is your effect on them. Giving good attention to people makes them more intelligent. Poor attention makes them stumble over their words and seem stupid. Your attention, your listening, is that important.

We think we listen, but we don't. We finish each other's sentences, we interrupt each other, we moan together, we fill in the pauses with our own stories, we look at our watches, we sigh, frown, tap our finger, read the newspaper, or walk away. We give advice, give advice, give advice. Even professional listeners listen poorly much of the time. They come in too soon with their own ideas. They equate talking with looking professional.

We all know what genuine listening looks like and feels like, because when we have been the receiver of it, it has stuck with us. It looks like eyes on our eyes, a welcoming face, a body turned toward us, waiting in ease and with encouragement and appreciation. It feels like a bosomy hug, a plate of warm chocolate chip cookies, and a tall glass of cool milk at Grandma's house—all loving and welcoming and "tell me all about it." True listening is pure magic.

We have found that when we move beyond superficial listening to genuine and loving attention, we receive more and those telling their stories give more. Our listening "grows" the quality and quantity of human experience available to be shared. If it is true, as Maya Angelou says, "[t]hat there is no agony like bearing an untold story inside of us," we believe it likewise true that there is no joy like being the midwife who draws that untold story forth from another and who hears it draw its first breath and come to life in the outside world.

Sometimes we assist others by listening to their stories. At other times, we give our greatest aid by telling them one of ours. "If stories come to you, care for them. And learn to give them away where they are needed. Sometimes a person needs a story more than food to come alive." (Barry Lopez) Scott learned this first-hand many years ago. He shares this story:

When I was in my early 30s and living in Dallas, Texas, I got swept up in a business deal that seemed too good to be true and, as it turned out, was nothing but a major swindle. I fell victim to a very slick and experienced con man, to the tune of hundreds of thousands of dollars.

This was totally devastating to me. My whole future looked bleak and hopeless. I had let my family down and my partners. I was the smart, young lawyer and I should have known better. My self-esteem was crushed. I felt stupid and vulnerable.

For weeks, I prayed and paced the floor and barely slept. I was irritable and short-tempered with my wife and young children. I found comfort in the Lord, but not resolution. I was embarrassed for anyone to find out about it, and yet I could not bear to carry the burden all by myself. Finally I felt impressed that I should talk with Tom Nelson.

Tom was a retired Navy pilot and a successful businessman. He was also my bishop and a dear friend. He had put a lot of trust and confidence in me, and I worried whether he could ever trust me again once I told him what I had done. With a great deal of anxiety, but feeling I had no other choice, I made an appointment to see him.

That meeting was a turning point in my life. Tom is a man of great love and great energy and great faith, and I was nourished by all three that day. We prayed together and counseled together, but the thing that touched me most was Tom's story. As I shared with him what had happened and how I felt, Tom said, "I think I know very well how you feel. In fact, I feel impressed to share with you something I wrote many years ago, when I was about your age. It's something I've never shared with anyone before, but I think I was guided to write it many years ago so that I could share it with you today."

Tom turned around in his chair to his credenza and pulled from the shelf a thick, black journal he kept. He thumbed through the pages until he found the spot he was looking for, and then started to read aloud to me: "August 17, 1962. My life has felt like a deep, dark hole the past several weeks, due to my own stupidity . . ."

I couldn't believe it! His story was just like mine! He too had been swindled, had felt the same despair I had felt. He too had wondered how he would ever face others, how he would ever dig himself out of the pit he was in, how he would ever get his life back on track. He too had let his fear and self-loathing ruin the way he treated his family. He too had turned to the Lord and had been guided to seek counsel from someone he loved and respected. And then he had found the faith and courage to keep going.

When I heard his story and saw that he had survived a huge body-blow, and that even with such a major misstep early in life, he had fought back and had become successful in so many ways, it gave me hope and courage. I knew the way would likely be long and hard, but because Tom had done it, I felt confident that I could come back too.

I'll always be grateful to Tom Nelson and his story. Tom Nelson's story was the lifeline that kept me from drowning in a sea of hopelessness. Tom Nelson's story saved my life.

It is true—sharing our stories matters, and sometimes we do need a story more than we need food. We need to tell our own stories, and we need to hear others' stories. For us, this is one of the greatest joys in life. ∞

CHAPTER 5

SHARING AND SAVING YOUR STORIES MATTERS

"TELL YOUR TALES; MAKE THEM TRUE.
IF THEY ENDURE, SO WILL YOU."
— JAMES KELLER

I f a story is worth sharing, we believe it is certainly worth saving. If *shared stories* are the threads in the ties that connect us person to person, then *saved stories* are the links in the chains that bind families over generations and entire cultures over centuries. If sharing our stories matters deeply—and we believe strongly that it does—then saving those stories matters just as much.

It is our experience that within each of us is an inner desire to make a difference in the lives of those around us and to leave a trace of ourselves when we leave this world. In typical Benjamin Franklin style, the editor of *Poor Richard's Almanac* gave this advice on the subject:

If you would not be forgotten,
As soon as you are dead and rotten,
Either write things worth the reading,
Or do things worth the writing.

We have found that sharing and saving our stories is the most immediate way of making a difference in the lives of others and leaving a trace of ourselves. Richard Stone eloquently captured this concept when he wrote, "At the end of lives, after we have passed on, all that is left of us is our story. In a peculiar way, these stories are our ticket to immortality. Knowing that future generations will retell our stories liberates us into a realm of timelessness."

During one of his storytelling classes, Richard was able to help one of his students understand the importance of passing on stories. He shares this story:

> Some years ago when I was teaching an Elderhostel course, a participant approached me following the class. She wanted some advice. Her husband had died six months before, leaving explicit directions in his will that she spend $3,000 to publish his life story. She was angry and confused by his request that she waste money on something so inconsequential. Who would want to read the idle chatter of an old man whose life had been so ordinary? She wasn't even certain that her children would be interested. It wasn't a great piece of literature, and was only fifty pages long. "Why would he do such a thing?" she asked.
>
> After spending three days in the course discovering and sharing her own life story, she had her answer. Standing before the class with tears in her eyes, she spoke of her love for her husband, and how he had loved her and their daughters. She also told the class the story of his life, his bequest, and how over the last four days her anger had been transformed into gratitude. By finally accepting the gift of his story and sharing it with others, she granted him not only his wish, but also a form of immortality. Who would have thought there was something so powerful in a simple tale waiting to be told? (Richard Stone, *The Healing Art of Storytelling*)

Finding ways to preserve and pass on our life learning and expressions of our love is a gift of immense service to many, including some we do not know or who may not even be alive yet. "Stories are love gifts," wrote Lewis Carroll. Scott was the recipient of such a gift from his mother. He shares this story:

My mother died of cancer when she was 32 years old, and I was eight, the oldest of her six surviving children. When I turned 12, my father took me aside and said, "Scott, I have something for you from your mother." Then he handed me a two-page letter that she had written to me not long before she passed, leaving instructions for my father that it be given me on my twelfth birthday, an age marking a rite of passage into manhood in our family's faith.

My mother's words of love, tenderness and wise counsel, penned in that brief letter, touched me to the core, and continue to do so now, decades later. She talked to me about making good choices in my teenage years, and the importance of staying close to family and friends. She told me how much she cherished our faith, and she expressed a deep hope that I would continue to value it, too. Most of all, she wanted me to know that, whatever choices I might make in my life, she would always love me.

I did not inherit any money or property from my mother. What little my parents had materially was spent on my mother's long and arduous medical treatment. To this day, however, I value that letter immeasurably, more than anything financial she could have left me. It is living proof that, even in her hour of suffering, knowing that she would not live to see me grow up, she thought of me, loved me, and found a way to make sure I knew it.

I remember too vividly how frail and thin she was at the end, her body emaciated by the cancer, as though it were physically drawing her from this world. Sometimes I imagine how hard she struggled to finish the six letters she knew she had to write before her strength abandoned her entirely. Now that I am the parent of six children, I think about her emotions as she fought to pen the last paragraphs, perhaps the last words of my letter. And I'm beginning to understand just how much her example of courage, love, heroic devotion, and selflessness mean to me and those around me.

Scott was recently reminded of the magnitude of his mother's gift.

I was speaking on the phone a few months ago with a professional colleague from Chicago. The subject of legacy building came up, so I told her about my experience receiving my mother's letter. As I shared my story with her, she noticed and commented on several significant parallels between her life and mine.

"My mother died of cancer when I was eight years old," I told her.

"Oh, how interesting," she said, "my mother died of cancer when I was seven years old."

"I was the oldest of six children" I continued.

"How uncanny," she observed, "I was the oldest of five children."

"When I was 12, my father gave me a letter my mother had written shortly before her death. It told how much she loved me and what she hoped I would remember about her, and it gave me wonderful advice about coping with the teenage years and holding on to the things that matter most."

There was a long and awkward silence on the other end of the phone. Finally, in a halting voice brimming with emotion, I heard her say, more to herself than to me, "Oh, how I wish I had a letter from my mother. . . ."

Taking the time and going to the trouble to save and pass on stories can be a service of inestimable value, especially among families. Stories are the connective tissue within and between generations. "Families are united more by mutual stories—of love and pain and adventure—than by biology. 'Do you remember when...' bonds people together far more than shared chromosomes. Stories are thicker than blood." (Daniel Taylor) Mary Lou James of Ocala, Florida, shares this heart-touching story about her father, who recently passed away.

I attended the Legacy Builder Retreat in August of 2007 and was inspired to approach my father about recording some of his stories. Dad was 83 at the time and a noncompliant insulin diabetic who was living on borrowed time with his health. Even though some of his other thought process had slowed down, he could still recall intimate details of his past. I sat with him and a digital recorder in my parents' assisted living facility apartment and together we captured stunning memories of his childhood, his experiences as a togelier on 36 B-17 combat missions over Italy during World War II, and recollections of his professional life as a chemical engineer. It was wonderful!

In February, I attended the Legacy Builder Retreat again with a friend and professional colleague. My participation in the program was frequently interrupted as I spent time on the phone from Orlando getting him moved out of the hospital/rehab and into hospice care. When I returned home, I sat with him for the next three days while he was at a hospice care center before he became unconscious. I was again able to record great memories of his life with my Mom, us kids, the war, and his employment years. It was an incredible way to fill the hours as we sat by his bedside waiting for him to cross over to the other side. Instead of a death watch, we filled the days with laughter and tears and joyful memories.

Of all his children, I was probably the closest to my Dad. After his death, my sister called me and said that now he was gone, she would have to get to know Dad through my eyes. Fortunately I am able to transfer the memories we captured onto a CD and share them with her, her daughter, and other members of the family. I am also going to write down stories of some of the great adventures Dad and I had together while they are fresh in my mind.

I'm so thankful I had the training and the tools to capture stories and memories of my Dad. He was my hero and now I have not only the personal memories of our time together but also recordings of his life experiences in his own voice.

It is encouraging to see people like Mary Lou take the initiative and find wonderful ways to preserve and pass on family stories, and we are impressed by the creativity and energy some show in finding ways to do so. Jeffrey Knapp of Basking Ridge, New Jersey, attempted to capture some of the stories of Chuck Hennigan, his retired engineer father-in-law, before he passed away about a year ago. Jeff shares this story:

I had suggested an interview or two to capture some of Chuck's wisdom and favorite stories, particularly for his grandchildren, who range in age from two to twenty. Chuck consistently postponed these interviews, feeling that there was "plenty of time" to do that. That "plenty of time" was cut short dramatically when Chuck fell and broke his hip, requiring major surgery and difficult rehabilitation. He became much more sedentary and his COPD flared up, resulting in difficulty breathing. Chuck became very weak, unable to share stories even in short snippets. In his final months, Chuck was confined to a hospice bed, cared for by Marie, his loving wife of fifty-plus years, his children, and an attentive home health aide. Three weeks from the first anniversary of his passing, we miss Chuck terribly; and I am thinking that hearing a few of his favorite anecdotes in his own voice would have brightened what will be an otherwise tough day for the family.

When we lost Chuck, I resolved to find a way to capture the history of my grandfather, John Gordon, who was my favorite storyteller and practical joker of all time. "PopPop" was still full of life and fun in his early nineties, pulling pranks that my two older boys, then preschoolers, can still remember fifteen years later. Unfortunately, my two younger boys just missed the antics of PopPop before he passed.

Since we can no longer interview him, I came up with the idea of preparing a script for my wife to interview *me* about my PopPop memories. Thus it became my job to recount the good times we spent together in my youth, plus what I know—and what would otherwise be lost forever—about how PopPop grew up. The highlight of this interview was the segment when I told the stories, in David Letterman countdown style, of "PopPop's Top Ten Practical Jokes." We were laughing and crying so hard we could hardly finish the interview. And even though we don't have PopPop's own voice, we were able to reconstruct a few of the volumes from the PopPop library.

Benjamin Light of Cleveland, Ohio, has found a delightful and imaginative way to remember his father. Each spring, normally on April 23, Ben hosts "Morton S. Light Baseball Day." In advance of the occasion, he sends a message to a number of his friends, clients, and family members, in which he relates the story behind the event. We share this from his message for 2008:

This April 23 my father would have turned 70. Before I go on, I want to take a moment to imagine what he would have been doing if he were alive today. I believe he still would have been working. Probably part-time and definitely only a few days a week but he loved being a pediatrician, and I cannot imagine he would have been able to say goodbye to the practice of medicine. I also believe he would have been teaching. He began his career in academic medicine and it makes sense to me that he would have shared his lifetime of experience with young doctors who were eager to learn. My father also loved to study and I think he would have continued to study his religion, his profession, and any other subjects that held his attention. Finally, I believe he would have enjoyed time with his family.

Although my daughter Hannah never knew my father, we speak about him often. He would have made the ideal grandfather: doting on her at every opportunity, undermining the authority of her parents, and generally enjoying the force of nature that is my almost five year old. It is the last part that is always the hardest for me to accept.

Last year, Morton S. Light Baseball Day saw a record number of attendees. Twenty people shared a cool Chicago evening and watched the Cubs once again snatch defeat from the jaws of victory. Young Prince Fielder hit two home runs, the second of which sunk the Cubs in extra innings. I only saw the first one because Hannah was making her inaugural trip to the game and in the middle of the eighth inning when she looked up at me and said, "Daddy can we go now?" I could not say no. She enjoyed the company, the food, the celebration of my father, a trip down onto the field and a little bit of baseball. We talk about it often and she cannot wait to go again this year.

For those who regularly receive this email and celebrate Passover (which is many), you are aware that Morton S. Light Baseball Day, my annual trip to see the Cubs in memory of my father, sometimes occurs in the middle of the Jewish celebration of the exodus from Egypt. Eight years ago, nine of us sat in the upper deck at Shea Stadium and ate hot dogs with no buns (although I do not believe the hot dogs were Kosher so one might ask why we clung so strongly to one tradition while ignoring another). However, this email is not about analyzing the way in which I practice my Judaism but about celebrating the life of my late father, Morton S. Light.

I included in this email my comments about Passover to explain why this year, for only the second time since I started this tradition in 1998, I will attend a Cubs game on a day other than April 23. This year, Jamie, Hannah and I are traveling to Chicago to break matzah with family and instead of coming home Monday and turning around again on Wednesday and heading to Denver, we are staying in Chicago and celebrating Morton S. Light Baseball Day on Monday, April 21. I think it is a decision my father would support.

For the first time since I began this tradition, I want to make a request of those who are kind enough to take the time to read this email. Although it has always been implied, I have never specifically asked people to use my method of staying connected to my father as a motivation for thinking about how you might stay connected to a lost loved one. I began this tradition to make my father's birthday something I looked forward to instead of dreading. It worked. I encourage everyone who reads this to take a moment and think if there is a way, big or small, that you can stay connected to someone who is no longer with you and make your feelings of loss a little easier to handle. I also encourage everyone to take the time to share with those closest to you how you want to be remembered when you are gone. It might make people feel better about engaging in the things you enjoyed when you are no longer there to participate.

I look forward to seeing those who can attend inside the Friendly Confines of Wrigley Field on April 21, 2008.

We think Ben has come up with a wonderful idea, and we echo his invitation for all of us to find a fun and loving way to stay connected to those who are no longer with us.

Robert Kwiatkowski of Springfield, Virginia, is taking a more traditional approach to saving and sharing family stories. Bob is writing a book entitled *Four Roses*. It spans three generations and tells about four women who have graced his life. He shares this story:

When my mother passed away from ovarian cancer, my three siblings and I each received a letter from her. Each letter started the same, "I love all of my children equally, but for different reasons."

She personalized each letter with why she loved each one of us so much. This letter was the most precious gift I received from my mother and it is one that I still cherish. The letter moved me, and still does. I carry it with me each day and re-read it occasionally for inspiration. My mother has inspired me to create a special legacy for my adopted daughter, Emily Rose. I am in the process of writing a book titled, *Four Roses.*

Growing up in New York City, my mother, Rosemary Kwiatkowski, was my biggest fan and supporter. I called her my "Sugar Mommy." Every time I did something good like get an "A" on a paper, a scholarship, a track medal, etc. she would praise me, tell everyone in the family, and at times get a clip in the local newspaper. The more she praised the more I liked it, and the more I tried to accomplish. Although I was one of the youngest in my family, with her encouragement, I become the first person to graduate college and the first person to get a masters degree.

As a family of six, we lived paycheck to paycheck. Our apartment in New York City was about 800 square feet. My brother and I, and my two sisters, slept in the same room in two bunk beds with a sheer curtain separating us. Due to my father's alcoholism we did not have a car. Up through college, I was out of New York City just two times: once on a bus trip to New Jersey for a church picnic, and once on a bus trip to Florida for an actual vacation. My Mom encouraged me not only to get my college degree but also to leave New York City, and I did both. I graduated as a Distinguished Graduate of the Air Force R.O.T.C. program at Manhattan College, and for the next twenty years my wife Roseann and I lived and traveled around the world.

Mom was the central figure in our family. My brother, sisters, and I did not really need to call each other since we got all the details from our calls to our Mom. This went on for a few decades until my Mom was diagnosed with ovarian cancer and died within a year. I know that my Mom loved us and was proud of us, which in turn made us proud to have such a caring and inspirational person as our mother. I am who I am today largely because of my Mom's influences.

There is no doubt in my mind that from heaven my Mom helped bring our daughter, Emily Rose, into our lives. It took ten years for the adoption to take place. Since I was in the military, every time we got close to getting a chance to adopt, we got reassigned and virtually had to start over again with the adoption process. Finally, however, the miracle occurred and Emily Rose entered our lives and magnificently changed our lives forever. After my wife Roseann and I read Emily Rose's background information from Catholic Charities, we knew, without a doubt, that my Mom had her hand in providing this wonderful child to us.

Roseann, really, really, really wanted to have a little girl. And after a ten year journey of ups and a lot of downs, our dreams came true. Interestingly, Emily Rose arrived simultaneously with our getting a new house and my getting a new job. I commented to Roseann, "A new baby, a new house, a new job—life doesn't get much better than this." Shortly after I said that, Roseann was diagnosed with thyroid cancer. A year later she was diagnosed with non-Hodgkins lymphoma. Another year later she was diagnosed with breast cancer. Six months later she died of cardio-myopathy. Emily Rose was just three and a half years old.

On Roseann's death bed, she asked one of her best friends, Rosemarie, to stay in Emily Rose's life. Rosemarie was a flight attendant and was living in Tennessee but commuted from Dulles airport in Virginia, close to where Emily Rose and I live. Between flights, Rosemarie would help me with Emily Rose as I adjusted to being a single parent. After connecting some dots, I realized that Roseann, like my Mom, was still helping me and caring for me even after she was physically gone. Rosemarie and I fell in love and a year after Roseann's passing, I married Rosemarie, and she adopted Emily Rose as her daughter. Life became good again. Emily Rose now has a 32 year old brother and is part of a very large family. Since Emily Rose is a gregarious person and a budding actress and singer, she loves the attention and is thriving, just the way Roseann wanted her to.

Although my Mom passed about 20 years ago, she still has a tremendous impact in my life in many ways. One of those ways is in writing. My Mom was a frustrated writer. She wrote several stories and sent them to Reader's Digest. Although she was never published, she liked to write and by my watching her, I was inspired to start to write my book, *Four Roses*.

The inspiration for my book comes from these four wonderful people in my life, for without them, I am not sure if I would be here today. I certainly would not be the person who I am today. Therefore, the book is to honor the memories of my precious Rosemary and dear Roseann, a thanksgiving for Rosemarie for turning her life upside down for Emily Rose and myself, and as a legacy to the precious little girl of ours—Emily Rose.

I hope this book, which will be filled with life lessons learned during the journey from love, to hope, to despair, to euphoria, to tragedy, to recovery, and then to renewal, will inspire others in coping with their lives. And I hope it moves them in some way to capture "their story" before it is too late. I've learned that tomorrow may never come.

We're certain Bob's book will be a wonderful blessing for his daughter Emily Rose. Reconnecting with family stories is a critical ingredient in helping today's youth understand their place in the universe. "Hearing and telling stories about their own family and heritage helps kids figure out how they fit in—at home and in the world." (Holly George Warren) This is a profoundly important part of their learning that can't be acquired in day care, at school, or anywhere else besides our homes. At least one author believes hearing family stories gives children a powerful sense of self-worth. "By hearing the emblematic tales that spring from your heart and your love, your child will sense his or her own worthy being in your eyes, and perhaps sense a worthiness in the broader scope of the human race." (Chase Collins)

The secret to transmitting family values to future generations is to find ways to make sure they hear the stories in which those values are imbedded. "Without preaching or moralizing, stories sum up our beliefs and principles. And there's no better way to communicate your family's values—whatever they may be—than to create and tell tales to your children." (Chase Collins) More than anyone else in the world, sharing and saving our stories ultimately matters most to members of our families.

We're often asked what method we recommend for sharing and saving stories. As may be obvious from some of the varied and ingenious ideas mentioned above, our answer is: WHATEVER WORKS FOR YOU! Whether it's personal letters, recordings, video tapes, compilations of sermons, collections of family recipes, journals, books, or even annual baseball days, the medium does not matter as much as the message. *How it is done* is not nearly as important as *that it is done.*

That said, we have observed that easier and simpler is usually better. The closer the method is to a plain old-fashioned heart-to-heart conversation, the more likely sharing and saving of stories will actually happen.

All it really takes are five basic things: 1) a handful of thoughtful story-leading questions; 2) a caring, attentive listener; 3) a comfortable place to sit and chat; 4) a few minutes of unrushed time; and 5) a dependable recording device. With those five ingredients, you've got the recipe for great story sharing and story saving just about every time.

Even though both of us are writers, and even though both of us have been richly blessed with written stories from our families, we must acknowledge that our first love is telling stories and listening to stories spoken aloud. There is something primeval and soul-satisfying in the oral sharing of stories. "Filling up blank sheets of paper is, indeed, not the same as the sound of your own voice in shaping a tale as it wells up out of your memory and as your own fancy plays with it with all its twists and turns. And the best part of it is that finally by some mysterious process you find that you are listening to the tale yourself as much as the listeners around you." (Richard Chase)

We love the magic that happens when a client, a family member, a friend, or even someone we barely know starts to remember events from their life and share them with us. We love to hear the energy in their voice as the saga unfolds. We love to watch their face as they talk about funny things, sad things, great successes, or colossal setbacks. We delight in noticing what words they choose to describe or explain something. It is indeed a magical moment for us to hear a story told aloud.

Scott's experience with a significant event in his grandfather's life is a great example of the power of oral histories. He shares this story:

My mother's father, "Grandpa Moody" as we called him, walked with a wooden leg. It wasn't one of those modern prosthetics of titanium but a heavy, clunky limb carved out of real wood. It fit over the 6-8 inch stump of his right leg and fastened around his waist with a thick leather belt. It didn't bend much at the knee, so he walked by planting his good left leg and then swinging his wooden leg, like Chester in the old *Gunsmoke* westerns, out and around in front of him.

With his grandchildren, Grandpa Moody was playful about his wooden leg. He could give us horsey rides for hours on that leg because it never got tired. On cool mornings he would teasingly put one of the white "stump stockings" that cushioned the nub of his right leg on his head like a ski cap. Occasionally, when he was working with a knife or ice pick, he would "slip" and stab himself in the leg, then scream in pain, then laugh his head off because he "gotcha."

It was always an adventure going anywhere with him in his old, red, stick-shift pickup. I was never clear how, in an era before automatic transmissions, he ever qualified for a driver's license. Since his good left foot had to push the clutch up and down, that left his wooden right foot to work both the gas and the brake. Whether it was lurching off and being pinned back against the seat when his wooden leg hit the accelerator, or wondering if we were going to stop as he was trying to swing that wooden leg over to the brake, there was seldom a dull moment with Grandpa Moody at the wheel.

The story of how he lost his leg was a piece of well-known, oft-repeated family legend, but one which, strangely, I never once heard him talk about. As a young father, a horse had rolled over on and crushed his right leg, requiring its amputation. While on the operating table, the doctors reported that they had "lost him" at one point during the surgery, but they were able to revive him. He reported that during that time, he experienced what many would call a "near-death experience," in which he felt that his spirit left his body and went to heaven, but he was sent back to complete his earthly mission.

Several years after his actual death, while I was in law school, a cousin let me listen to a tape recording he had found of someone interviewing Grandpa Moody about the events of that evening when he lost his leg. In his own words and in his own voice, he described in vivid detail the accident with the horse, the painful trip to the hospital, the fateful decision to remove his leg, the feeling of his spirit leaving his body on the operating table, and the exquisite beauty he saw in heaven. He recounted seeing his young son who had died earlier, and meeting old friends, some of whom were making flowers. He explained how it was determined that he should return to life, shared his very mixed feelings about "coming back," and told what it was like to return to the operating room and to his body.

It was, without a doubt, the most incredible narrative I have ever heard! The hair on the back of my neck was fully erect, and every particle of my body seemed to be engaged in listening to that old familiar voice telling what had happened to him on that evening long ago. It will live forever in my memory.

What was so eye-opening to me was to recognize that, while I was well-acquainted historically with the events of that evening, it was an experience of an entirely different magnitude to hear *him* tell what *he saw and heard and felt.* With his telling of the story, I WAS THERE. Listening to his words, I could see it through his eyes and hear it through his ears. I learned then that no one else can tell our stories like we can.

There's a bit of a sad ending to Scott's story: he never made a copy of that tape, and now, no one seems to remember what happened to it. He could kick himself for that, and he would give almost anything to have it back. What a treasure he and his family have lost.

We believe that saving our stories does matter. In the great circle of human ecology, stories are not intended to be spoken but once and then cast off. Like other living creatures, they are worthy of our best efforts to rescue them and safeguard them and send them forward to the next generation. When we keep the stories alive, we also keep alive the people who lived them.

CHAPTER 6

SHARING AND SAVING YOUR KEEPSAKE AND HOME-PLACE STORIES MATTERS

"FAVORITE PEOPLE, FAVORITE PLACES,
FAVORITE MEMORIES OF THE PAST.
THESE ARE THE JOYS OF A LIFETIME,
THESE ARE THE THINGS THAT LAST."

— HENRY VAN DYKE

Personal objects of deep emotional value and recollections of the places where we grew up are the reservoirs of some of the most important memories we have. Stories about these objects and places reside in a special place near our hearts. We call these stories "keepsake stories" and "home-place stories," and they deserve unique attention.

An ordinary, mundane object or photograph becomes a priceless treasure when it's the subject of a keepsake story. The dullest, most boring place on the planet becomes a Shangri-la when it's the subject of a home-place story. Stories make keepsakes and home places much more valuable.

In our work planning estates and helping families settle the affairs of deceased loved ones, we have learned that when keepsakes and home places are associated with the stories of a loved one, they are often considered the most precious portions of the estate, notwithstanding they have relatively little financial value.

Conversely, when the objects or the home places become separated from their defining stories, they revert to just being "stuff," valued at whatever they will fetch on the market. We have seen what might have been considered priceless pictures and heirlooms sold at garage sales for nickels and dimes, and we have seen old farms and home sites liquidated quickly for whatever they will bring. Their worth was limited to their "fair market value."

Scott used to work with a colleague who owned a powder horn that had been in his family since the Revolutionary War. Unfortunately, no one knew anything about its actual history: they didn't know who had used it or where or when. The powder horn and its story had become separated, and its value had plummeted. As far as the owner was concerned, he hoped it might be worth something on *Antique Roadshow*, but that was the extent of its value to him.

Steve Gammill from Fruita, Colorado, understands the impact of keepsakes and photographs when their stories are still associated with them. He shares this story.

In my conference room where I normally meet with clients, I have a number of wall hangings that are of particular importance to me. Some are photographs while others are actual keepsakes from my past; all take me back to meaningful experiences in my life.

One item was recently featured in our local newspaper when a reporter and photographer came out to interview Jan and me about our Legacy Building work. It's a framed piece of old, yellowed paper that I call "The Toy Tractor Mortgage." It's a vivid reminder of an important story that happened when I was nine years old.

The year was 1949 and we lived in the small town of McCook, Nebraska. My dad was the managing editor of the town's only newspaper, *The McCook Daily Gazette*. The newspaper office was downtown, right across the street from the dime store.

I was in the dime store one afternoon looking at toys and, to my delight I discovered a wonderful red tractor. It was plastic, dark red, and about eight or nine inches long and three or four inches high. It had black rubber treads and looked like a Caterpillar tractor, except it was red. It was love at first sight, and I knew I just had to have it. But then I looked at the price tag and my heart sank. It cost four dollars! Four dollars, and I only had three dollars to my name.

Sometimes desperate situations call for reckless behavior. I couldn't come up with any other plan except to go across the street to the newspaper office and ask my dad to help me out. I have no idea what I expected him to say or do. He was definitely not the kind to reach into his pocket and dole out money to his kids anytime they wanted something. But I only needed a dollar, so I thought that maybe, just this once, it wouldn't hurt to ask.

He was in his office wearing his white shirt and tie with his sleeves rolled up and working away on something. I don't remember the conversation or how I pitched it, but I do remember that all of a sudden, he turned to his typewriter without saying more and started to type.

I wish I could describe the sound that typewriter made when he inserted the paper and rolled that black roller so that the paper was ready to receive the striking keys. His typewriter was a large manual, typical of what might be found in a newspaper office of that era. I remember that it made a lot of noise, a loud rhythmic clacking noise. My dad was a superb typist and he could make that typewriter sing! Those keys sang "clickety-clack, clickety-clack" and there was always that "ding" when the typewriter reached the right margin. Then the "clickety-clack" would halt briefly while dad reached up with his left hand and pushed back the carriage, using the silver return lever. Then the rhythmic "clickety-clack" would begin again.

In no time he was finished typing. Pulling the paper from the machine, he handed me what was titled "Chattel Mortgage." It was two short paragraphs, double spaced and essentially said that I acknowledged borrowing one dollar from the "party of the first part, Kenneth A. Gammill" and promising, as the "party of the second part," to repay "said debt on or before Sunday, July 3rd, 1949, along with five cents interest." Failing to do so, it went on, would result in the release of possession and title to the tractor until such time as the debt had been paid or some other event had occurred "at the discretion of the party of the first part."

Beneath all those "whereases" and "parties of the first part" and "parties of the second part" was a place for us both to sign, which we did. My little sister must have been with me or at least readily available because she signed as a witness.

Looking back, I can remember playing with the red tractor out in the front yard where I had quite a structure built in the dirt for my toy cars and trucks. And although I don't have a clear recollection of paying the debt or of having the tractor repossessed, I'm quite certain, knowing my dad, that I did in fact pay the debt in full and on time. It was a powerful lesson for a nine-year-old boy.

We love how Steve uses "The Toy Tractor Mortgage" and its accompanying story to introduce himself and tie together his small-town roots, his family connections, his life story, his work as an attorney, his work as a Legacy Advisor, and the important values of keeping your word, being creative, and finding resourceful ways to solve problems. It's hard to imagine a more effective way of sharing who he is and how he intends to care for his clients. It's a great example of the power of a keepsake story.

Keepsake stories preserve the value of sentimental items like "The Toy Tractor Mortgage," as well as the people associated with them.

Without the story, that old yellow paper is probably headed for the trash as soon as Steve is gone. With the story, both the paper and Steve live on.

Bradley Hahn of Mesa, Arizona, uses his own stories and experiences to teach these principles to his clients. He shares this story:

I was recently working with an older couple who had immigrated to Arizona from Germany. When I asked them what plans they had for their keepsake items, they seemed discouraged. The wife said, "We have a wonderful set of china we've used during all our children's lives for special occasions. I got the set from my mother back in the old country, and she got it from her mother, and it has a lot of history. However, when I mentioned it to my children, they didn't seem to care at all. They said it's too much trouble. We feel very put off by their attitudes and we don't know what to do about it now."

I asked them if their children understood the story behind the china. The wife got quiet and said she didn't think so.

I said, "Well, let me share something with you. When I was back visiting my grandma in Nebraska, I told her that she should start passing down some of the heirlooms she had that meant a lot to her."

She said, "Oh, I don't have much of anything, and besides, the kids have already said they're not interested in it. They've already got plenty of furniture and don't need anything of mine."

I walked over to a drawer, pulled out a rosary I knew was there, and said to her, "Grandma, tell me about this rosary."

She said, "Well that particular rosary belonged to my parents and they used it every day back in Germany. Originally it was the rosary given to my great-grandfather at his first communion as a young man."

"Wow," I said to her, "that's incredible. Do your children know that story?"

She said she didn't think so.

"Well, Grandma, how about if you tell me more about this rosary and I write down its history and anything else you know about it and then I send the story around to your kids along with the rosary, and let's see what happens. Would that be OK with you?" I asked.

She said, of course, that would be fine, so we did that. In very short order, once her children (my aunts and uncles) understood the story behind that rosary, they became very interested, not only in it, but in lots of other keepsakes she wanted them to have. It changed their whole perspective.

When I finished telling my clients about my experience with my grandma, I asked, "What do you think about trying something like that with your set of china, capturing the story and sharing it with your daughters?"

The wife replied, "Brad, I think that's a great idea. Let's try it and see what happens."

About a month later she called me back with a report. "Brad, thanks for your suggestion. I did what you said—I typed up the story of the china and sent it out to all the kids. Now *all* the kids want the china. I guess we need to send them the stories of lots of other keepsakes we have so they don't just focus on the china."

Chris Mares of Appleton, Wisconsin, learned from an experience in his own family how a story can turn what might appear to be an old piece of junk into a valuable treasure. With Chris, it was an old wooden buggy wheel. He shares this story:

I came darn close to throwing out the old buggy wheel, but now I'm really glad I didn't.

Every December for as long as I can remember, our family fashioned an old wooden buggy wheel four feet in diameter into a Christmas wreath and hung it up on stakes in our front yard. It always was a massive effort to haul the heavy wheel from the basement, replace the burned-out bulbs, re-tie the garland, carry it through the snow, and hang it on long steel stakes driven into the frozen Wisconsin ground.

As a child, I hated the cold and the work and especially having to hold the stakes while my father or older brother used a 30-pound stake driver to pound in the stakes. As an adult, I was never all that impressed with the wheel as a Christmas decoration. So when my mother was seriously ill in the hospital and I was taking care of her affairs, I thought it might be the right moment to see about heaving that old wooden wheel.

I casually brought up the subject of the wheel to my mother as she lay in the hospital and hinted that it might be time to do some cleaning. What she shared with me from her sickbed completely changed my ideas about jettisoning the wheel.

My mother told me that as the only daughter of the seven children in her family, she spent most of her time as a child and a teenager with her mother. On their farm, the boys were responsible for the outside farm chores, including milking the cows, and she was responsible to work with her mother to prepare meals, wash clothes, clean, and complete other household chores. Over the years of working together, the two of them became very close.

My mother remembers her mother in the buggy, going five miles each way to town to attend church or buy supplies at the store.

Those are precious memories of a special time in her life as a young Wisconsin farm girl, memories she still cherishes at her advanced age.

Eventually, though, the buggy was pushed aside in favor of a motor car, and then ultimately dismantled because it was in the way. But on a Depression-era farm, nothing was ever thrown away, since everything might have a use in the future. The buggy parts were saved, including the wheels, which were stored in the back of the haymow in the barn.

After my mother was married, she asked her father if she could have the wheels because they reminded her of her mother and their special mother-daughter relationship. Since by then the days of the horse-drawn buggy were long gone, he agreed to let them go.

Being a newlywed short on money but wanting a unique and festive Christmas decoration, my mother used garland and some big, old-fashioned outdoor colored lights to turn one of the wheels into a down-home wreath. That wheel became an important symbol for her, bridging both her love for her mother—my grandmother— and the holiday traditions she established in her own home.

As you might have guessed, hearing her story of the history of the buggy wheel changed its value entirely in my eyes. Once I understood its role in her life, it took on a completely new meaning to me.

Now the tradition of putting up the wagon wheel at Christmas time has passed to my son Kevin and me. Each December, after the snow has arrived in Wisconsin and the ground has frozen hard, Kevin and I get the old wooden buggy wheel out of storage and hang it up in front of my mother's house, and as we do, I tell him about a young Wisconsin farm girl and her mother riding in a two-wheel horse-drawn buggy, perhaps on a cold December day like this one. "That was your grandmother and great-grandmother," I tell him, "and this is one of the wheels on that buggy."

These kinds of stories, it seems to us, help close the circle of life. They draw families together and they teach family values. They give children and grandchildren a sense of belonging and a sense of their location in the constantly turning wheel of human history. Like the North Star, they help us all know where we are and where we should be headed.

Photographs

"A PHOTOGRAPH NEVER GROWS OLD."
—ALBERT EINSTEIN

One category of keepsakes deserves special mention: photographs. In some ways, photographs tell their own stories—remember, "a picture is worth a thousand words." We have learned that by adding a small amount of additional information, a photograph can be rich with meaning. Volumes can be triggered by a single old snapshot, and a whole library of stories can be contained within a small album of pictures.

However, without the story, even photographs become garage sale commodities. "A family's photograph album is generally about the extended family and, often, is all that remains of it." (Susan Sontag) When that happens, it becomes worthless. In our work settling estates, we have seen piles and piles of family photographs thrown in the trash because no one knew the stories and as a result, no one cared what became of the pictures.

One of the treasures in Scott's wife's family is seven identical files of photographs of family heirloom furniture taken by her father, Henry Ware Hobbs, Jr. Henry was a wise lawyer who had seen too often the ugly side of family fights over personal property after the death of parents or grandparents. He was determined that his niece and six children wouldn't be thrown into that same conflict when he passed away. He also loved history and stories, and he appreciated the value of keeping history and stories alive and connected to keepsakes and photographs.

One fall, several years before his untimely passing, Henry sent his six children and his niece each a long legal file captioned "Choose It or Lose It." The cover letter invited them to come to his house the day after Thanksgiving where they would draw numbers and proceed to select which pieces of heirloom furniture they wished to receive when he was gone. Inside each of the seven folders were photographs of each and every piece. Beside each photograph he had written the story of each article. Each item, he noted, had a history which he carefully laid out—how old it was, where it was made if he knew, how it had come into the family, who had owned it within the family, and how and where it had been used, together with any other interesting tidbits he could recall. The text for each piece of furniture is fascinating reading.

The "Choose It or Lose It" process Henry set in motion worked beautifully; over time, all Henry's personal possessions were amicably and equitably distributed. But one of the most valuable objects to come out of his creativity were the seven "Choose It or Lose It" folders them-selves, each one rich with photographs and stories about all the other treasures. Like a pirate's map leading the way to buried riches, those folders led the way to finding the value in each of the other objects. Like an old-fashioned turnkey, they opened the strongbox to the human wealth inherent in the rest of the collection. Who knew that a long legal file would one day hold such treasures?

The value of even a single photograph along with its story cannot be easily overstated. Gary Waitzman of Lincolnshire, Illinois, owns a keepsake photograph that recently came into his possession. Besides the phenomenal event portrayed in the picture, the story of how it came into Gary's hands is also quite remarkable. He shares this story:

In September 2007 my wife Katie and I took my first trip ever to Europe. We talked about visiting many different possible places but I told her for me a trip to Normandy was a must. I have always been a World War II buff and have long enjoyed movies and books on the topic. We took the train from Paris to Caen and as we got closer to the Normandy region I started getting goose bumps. We rented a car and as we started our drive out of Caen to our destination of Bayeux (the first town liberated by the Allies after the invasion) the realization of where I was really hit me for the first time.

The trip was nothing short of monumentally spiritual for me as I found an even deeper appreciation of what these men had accomplished for all of us today. I felt extremely fortunate to meet Don Millarkey (of Band of Brothers fame) while visiting the Airborne Museum in St. Mere Eglise, the small town where many paratroopers of the 82nd and 101st Airborne mis-dropped and were killed in the early fighting on June 6, 1944. While I loved the rest of the trip to Belgium and Amsterdam, the experience of Normandy will stay with me forever.

Upon returning, while talking with a cousin, I became aware of an 85-year-old uncle who had fought in Normandy and who knew a lot about the scenes I had just visited. For a variety of silly reasons, I had no previous relationship with Uncle Mort and I had not really spoken with him or his children for over 40 years. Yet I felt a sense of kinship to him, both because he was my father's youngest brother and because I had just been where he had been and those stories were very fresh and real to me. I decided to swallow my pride and call Uncle Mort and see if I could establish a connection after all these many years. To my relief and delight, both Uncle Mort and his wife, Aunt Aviva, received my call warmly and expressed their pleasure at my taking this step. Just that alone was a wonderful additional benefit of my trip to France.

Because of the tone of the phone call, I decided after a few months to dip my toe into the water a little deeper. I called Uncle Mort and Aunt Aviva and asked if I could visit them in Atlanta. They said of course that would be fine, so this year, over Passover, Katie and I and my grown daughter Jenny spent three wonderful days with my new old family (or is it my old new family?). Uncle Mort shared many very deep personal moments of events he experienced fighting in Normandy over 60 years ago. He cried and laughed as we talked about men who had died fighting alongside him, and people he had saved when he helped liberate their concentration camps.

Without a doubt, the highlight of Uncle Mort's war stories for me was when he gave me a picture of a group of fellow Jewish soldiers praying, but with a large swastika emblem on the wall behind them. It was a phenomenal occasion! His unit had captured the Nazi headquarters of propaganda minister Joseph Goebbels in the spring of 1945, shortly before Passover. He and a number of his Jewish colleagues and many concentration camp survivors they had liberated then celebrated Passover services in Goebbels' headquarters' main meeting hall. I nearly burst with pride listening to my Uncle's description of this monumental and symbolic accomplishment. I relive those feelings every time I see the photograph or tell someone about it.

Another high point of our visit to Atlanta was joining Uncle Mort and his family for Passover. I experienced an incredible feeling of family connection Saturday night as Katie, Jenny, and I were welcomed by my cousins to their family Seder to celebrate Passover together for the first time ever. I thanked everyone from the bottom of my heart for welcoming my family to theirs. Uncle Mort responded that everyone there was of the same family, and from the love we received from them, I felt the truth of his words as I have never before felt that feeling in my life.

I'm so grateful I took the trip to Normandy, which led to this wonderful healing with my family and which I may never have known otherwise. I'm already planning another trip to Atlanta because it's hard to catch up on 40 years in only three days. I'll always cherish this newfound connection, and I'll always cherish the photograph of a most unusual Passover in a time when faith and goodness triumphed over brute force and evil.

Gary's story illustrates a number of important points, one of which is the power of keepsake stories (as well as other types of stories) to teach values, build faith, heal old wounds, reunite families, and open lines of communication among generations. There is something very impactful about combining a story with a photograph or a keepsake; together they seem to create a synergy that is far more potent than either one by itself.

Because of the wealth of information already present in a photograph, it usually doesn't take much to keep the basic story alive. The "who," "when," "where," and "what" behind the picture can be preserved and connected to the photograph without too much work. We think it's a shame when people don't do something to protect this important part of the story.

Another fascinating aspect of photographs is their generative nature—their ability to be the catalyst for the development of lots of other stories. One way to spawn a number of wonderful stories is to sit with a family member or friend and a set of photographs from their lives, and to ask them to tell about the scenes documented in the pictures. Each of the primary stories engendered by the photographs will usually lead to another story and then another and then several more after that. With a recorder, a listening ear, and an hour or two, we think this would be a marvelous technique to help others share and save their stories.

Home-Place Stories

Home places are significant and meaningful so long as the stories remain attached to them, but once the story-links are broken, they become just another patch of ground. Much like photographs, home places and stories cross-pollinate each other. Stories bring home places to life and at the same time, home places give new life to stories, drawing them from deep storage in our minds, dusting them off, and releasing them to the world. Taking a family member or friend back to their home place will cause hundreds of stories to burst into bloom.

The issue with home-place stories is often not primarily our own personal sense of connection to the places where we grew up, but rather how to make those places meaningful to people we care about. Unless we block out the stories due to trauma or abuse or we choose to forget them, we usually remain in touch personally with our growing-up places. The challenge is when we attempt to connect others such as spouses, children, or grandchildren to home places where they have never lived. Without the stories, others perceive very little value in home places. Talking about them or the suggestion to go there is usually met with rolled eyes, bored yawns, or sighs of desperation. We have found, however, that when those people know the relevant home-place stories, such places come alive with meaning for them.

In our Legacy Builder work, we've had wonderful experiences taking people back to their home-place stories by asking them to draw a floor-plan of the home where they grew up, including garages, tree houses, basketball courts, pools, and other similar areas. If it's a multi-level house, we ask them to make a floor plan for each story. If it's an apartment, we ask them to add hallways, elevators, and other parts of the building. We tell them not to worry if their drawings aren't perfect; the principal purpose of the drawing is to help them remember.

Then we ask them to take us on a verbal tour of this home and, along the way, to share with us some of the events they remember happening at different places in the house or near it. After a bit of hesitation, they warm up and then start discovering that they've struck a mother lode of storytelling ore. There's a story in every room and more up in the tree house, down in the basement, and out in the barn. Often, clients are so full of energy it's hard to get them to end when time runs out.

Going back to one's home place can evoke volumes of memories and stories. It can sometimes be a little unsettling, as Ted Ripley of Port Angeles, Washington, learned recently. He shares this story:

> In preparation for a Legacy Builder training program, I read in *How to Say it to Seniors* that seniors sometimes go back and review earlier stages of their lives in order to sort out the meaning of their lives and determine how they want to be remembered. That idea got me thinking I should go back and visit the blueberry farm where I grew up near Kent, Washington.

> I hadn't been back to Kent for about 25 years, so my early morning drive there was filled with a flood of old memories. I recalled that in the 1950s, when I was 12 years old, my family moved from town to a blueberry farm on the east hill of Kent, 30 acres all together. I remembered that on my first birthday on the farm, I received a shiny red bike with a fresh coat of paint (as I was not the first owner). The bike may have been used, but it was my ticket to freedom. With it, I was able to ride to the lake for swimming, to go to the store to buy some treats, or to just get out and go. What a sense of independence!

I remembered how we soon discovered that blueberry farming is very hard work. Farming was actually a side project for my dad, since he worked full-time at Boeing as a machinist. The blueberry farm was a way of bringing in some extra income, and part of the plan was that this income would be used for my college education. As long as I could remember, there was an expectation that I would go to college, even though none of my five older brothers and sisters had, and even though I didn't know what I was going to become as a result of going to college. We just all understood that I was definitely going to go to college, and blueberries were going to pay for it.

I had lots of memories of my assigned project to expand the number of acres planted in blueberries. I worked long, back-breaking hours digging holes, transplanting, plowing, pruning, fertilizing and doing all that's involved in establishing a blueberry farm. I recalled picking blueberries with the rest of the crew when I was younger, and then as I grew older, being in charge of running the picking crew, driving the blueberries to the cannery, and learning all aspects of blueberry farming.

I remember going away to college and leaving the blueberries in my parents' care, but then after a year Merrily and I were married and we moved our 40 foot trailer to the blueberry farm where we lived as I commuted to school. We built a home on that property, then later sold it and moved closer to the University. We used the proceeds from the sale to help pay for the last two years of law school. These and many other memories were bursting into mind as I drove through the early morning darkness.

It was just getting light when I arrived at the blueberry farm. I parked at a neighbor's house and started walking up the long driveway, which was now paved. "That's different," I thought to myself. Then I came to a fence surrounding some houses where my horse pasture had been when I was a boy. "That's different too," I said to myself. Then in the dawn I saw the one-word sign on the fence that rattled me and forever altered my plans to walk around on the blueberry farm and recapture my childhood memories there. The sign read simply: "WETLANDS."

In the months that have passed since I returned to the blueberry farm, I have gained a little more perspective and a lot of insight about life. I now see clearly what I saw only dimly in the early morning light: Things do not remain the same. Things changed in my life and obviously things changed on the blueberry farm. What was then prime blueberry land is now preserved as wetlands for birds and other creatures. The upland part of the blueberry farm is now a well-developed community containing 30 or 40 houses. The farm is not the same; the world is not the same. Times change, and now it's time for me to think about preserving my stories and my memories so my grandchildren will have a better understanding of what it was like in the 1950s on a blueberry farm on the east hill of Kent, Washington.

As Ted's story illustrates, going back to our home places, whether physically or in our memories, is an important aspect of the life-review process. It helps us put together many of the disjointed pieces of our personal narrative, and see more clearly our role on the larger stage of life. The stories we discover there are rich and meaningful, worthy of sharing and saving.

Scott experienced the power of home-place stories in 2005 when he went with his father and several of his siblings to the tiny village where his father was born. He shares this story:

My dad was born in the village of Colonia Garcia, Chihuahua, Mexico, in 1929. Colonia Garcia was an American settlement high in the Sierra Madre Mountains southwest of El Paso, Texas. My great-grandfather was one of the original settlers in the early 1890s. The families there were ranchers and loggers, and my grandfather was a crackerjack guide for American hunting parties attracted by the bountiful wildlife in the rugged mountains.

My dad and his parents and 12 brothers and sisters left Colonia Garcia when he was seven years old, in order to find better educational and marital opportunities for their large family. They migrated in a pick-up and a covered wagon to Fruitland, New Mexico, where I was born and raised. He had been back a few times previously but I had never been there before. It turned out for me to be a trip of a lifetime.

Colonia Garcia is situated in a wide valley near the tops of the mountains. The distance from the town of Colonia Juarez at the base of the mountains to Colonia Garcia is only a couple of dozen miles, but the trek over the rugged road took more than three hours in a four-wheel-drive truck. At every stop and around every bend, my dad found another story in his memory and he was eager to share them.

"Oh, here is what they call 'Lover's Cave' because courting couples were said to come here to do a little smooching."

"This is the old wagon road where my dad and older brothers would bring timber off the mountain on horse-drawn carts. See how the iron wheels wore grooves into the rock?"

"This is where we forded this stream. During spring run-off, you could hardly get across because of the high water."

Once we got to what was left of the village itself, Dad took us on a guided tour of all the places he remembered and shared more stories about each one.

"The church was here, which is also where we went to school."

"Uncle Earl's house was over there, and this is where they had a little store."

"I remember horse races between the mountain folks and the town folks right along here on the main street."

We found my great-grandfather's grave and another near-by grave where a family of cousins had buried five babies all below the age of two. He told about how hard it was to get medical care high up in the mountains, so when a child got very sick, it was almost always fatal.

He took us to the now-empty lot where their family home once stood and paced off the dimensions of the house. He explained the lay-out of the rooms inside and pointed out where the barns and other out-buildings were located. We dug up clay bricks from the foundation to take home with us, keepsakes of a special, almost sacred, place. It was a profound and touching experience for him and all of us.

That night we camped out in a rough cabin near his birthplace. Around the fire, we heard more wonderful, incredible stories. One in particular that I shall never forget was about a time when he went along with his father while his father felled trees for their lumber operation.

"I was about six years old and it was a special treat to get to go along with my dad," he said. "My dad was an excellent woodsman, very handy at felling trees with an ax and a saw, and expert at making them fall precisely where he wanted them to land. He had positioned me away from him, out of harm's way."

"Then at the moment the tree started to fall, the wind shifted sharply and my dad realized that the giant pine tree was headed toward me. I was in grave danger."

"'Marion,' he shouted at me, 'get behind that big tree right beside you! Hurry! Hurry!'"

"I started immediately to follow my father's orders, when in a flash, a voice I recognized as the Holy Spirit whispered to me, 'No, don't go behind that tree. Run, Marion, run away as fast as you can!'"

"In that split-second, I made the determination to obey the Spirit and not my father. I ran as fast as my little six-year-old legs could carry me, away from the crashing pine tree."

"I was able to get out of the way, and when the dust settled, I looked back to see what had happened. As it turned out, when the tree fell, it hung up partially on another tree and then rolled. As it crashed to the ground, its largest branch came slicing down along the back of the very tree where my father had told me to go. If I had been there, I would have been crushed to death instantly."

He paused and looked slowly around the fire at us to make sure he had our attention. "All my life, since I was six year old, I have known that there is safety in following the whisperings of the Spirit. I hope you will always remember what I have told you. You will be safe if you learn to listen to the Spirit."

My dad is gone now. Without him, and given the difficulty of the trip, I doubt many of us will ever get back to Colonia Garcia. But those memories and his stories now live on in each of us who were with him there. They must not remain locked away inside of us. We now have a responsibility to safeguard what we heard and felt and to share it with his grandchildren and great-grandchildren. Our telling of his stories keeps him and his wisdom alive.

Home-place stories and keepsake stories are unique treasures in our storehouses of personal and family stories. These stories and the keepsakes, photographs, and home places they spring from are deeply symbiotic, giving each other strength and helping each other grow in value. The abundant harvest resulting from this cross-pollination must be gathered in, savored in the present, and preserved for our future nourishment. ᧚

CHAPTER 7

SHARING YOUR STORIES WITH YOUR ADVISOR MATTERS

"WHEN A PROFESSIONAL ADVISOR
AND A CLIENT SIT DOWN TOGETHER
TO BEGIN PLANNING,
THERE ARE TWO EXPERTS
IN THE ROOM, NOT JUST ONE."

— NANCY KLINE

In the right hands, our personal stories can help create the best estate planning and financial planning services available anywhere. This remarkable "technology" is called **story-based planning**.

Many people are surprised to learn that their personal stories can help guide their financial advisor to the best investments, the best financial plan, the best retirement plan, and the best insurance products for them. They are equally surprised to hear that their personal stories can help their attorney design and draft the best wills and trusts, the best estate plan, and the best business succession plan for them and their families.

We think story-based planning represents the future of planning. Fortunately, it is already available from a growing number of visionary and forward-thinking professional advisors in many parts of the country.

Story-based estate planning and financial planning are the best ways to leverage the value of both our financial and non-financial wealth, and to create a better life and legacy for ourselves and those we love. The experience of working with a financial advisor or estate planner who understands the significance of sharing and savings stories is richly meaningful, enjoyable, and effective.

Traditional financial planning and estate planning can be a rather dreary process. Sometimes it's downright intimidating. The focus on numbers, documents, products, death, taxes, legal minutiae, and similar issues make it difficult to grasp and unpleasant to deal with. It's not surprising that a majority of Americans have never done any planning, and that the plans of those who have are typically inappropriate or out of date.

By comparison, story-based planning is rich with meaning, is pleasant and engaging, and is more likely to produce the results that matter most to clients. This is clearly the case when it is delivered by an advisor who personally understands the importance of stories, and who has the skills and tools to elegantly and seamlessly weave story into the process along with the more traditional elements of planning, such as investments, insurance, taxes, legal documents, public benefits, and charitable giving.

Story-based planning is meaningful.

Story-based planning is more meaningful for the client because it begins with the discovery of the client's values rather than with a listing of how much the client is worth and where those assets are positioned. The central question is "Who are you and what do you value?" rather than "What does your balance sheet look like?"

This discovery process, as it turns out, uses the most natural and effective methodology available—tapping into the client's stories—to uncover and clarify the client's values, rather than a multi-page questionnaire. A story-based discovery process is more organic and less contrived than a questionnaire-driven one. Traditional planners like multi-page questionnaires because they deliver cut-and-dried, categorical answers, more along the lines of their traditional training. The trouble is, none of us as a person is cut and dried and categorical, and none of us has a value structure that is cut and dried and categorical. We are full of nuances, contradictions, uncertainties, places where the lines are blurred. Traditional planners have a hard time with that; story-based planners relish the uniqueness of each individual and each family.

Traditional planners like multi-page questionnaires because they don't require that the planner listen respectfully and attentively to the clients. The "correct answer" or the client's "category" just pops out from an analysis of the questionnaire. Story-based planning, on the other hand, requires careful and attentive listening on the part of the advisor. Each client story is laced with insight and meaning, each story full of clues and pieces of answers. Real people living real lives are like that—the right answers don't just pop out; they have to be pieced together like a jigsaw puzzle.

Another problem with questionnaires is that by their nature they have the biases of their creators built into them. We've seen long, beautiful, and well-worded questionnaires that were intended to assess a client's "values" and direct the planner to the type of plan the client needed. Oddly, however, it seemed that nearly everyone using that questionnaire was steered toward essentially the same plan, one that favored the aims and products promoted by the questionnaire designer. We told the clients who asked us about it, "When everyone gets the same answer, maybe they're asking the wrong questions." With a story-based discovery process, each person's unique set of stories leads to a unique design, custom-built for them.

Stories are the best, most authentic tool for discovering the meaning of the core pieces of the design foundation for each client. In financial plans and estate plans, the client's meaning of money is a key piece of the foundation. That's because the meaning of money is as unique and personal to each of us as our fingerprints. It is something we have acquired through a lifetime of experiences with money. Then in turn, like it or not, our lives become significantly defined by what money means to us. It shapes our personal identity, our relationships, our careers. It affects our sense of the past, our awareness of the present, and our vision of the future.

In our opinion, no one should consider entrusting their money to someone who doesn't really understand what money means to them. Whether we're considering leaving money to children, grandchildren, or a charitable organization; or we're about to turn over investment assets to a financial advisor; or we're asking someone to help us make estate or financial plans, we should share our wealth only with those who are privy to the meaningful experiences that have shaped *our* understanding of what money is all about.

Those who would inherit our money need to know what it took to earn it and safeguard it, and they need to hear in our own words the lessons life has taught us about how to use wealth wisely. When an inheritance is combined with the wisdom to use it wisely, it can become a meaningful and lasting legacy.

Those who would manage or plan for our money need to appreciate the experiences that have influenced our sense of what money really stands for. They need to understand how it fits in with the larger themes of our lives.

The best way for them to understand what money means to us is by hearing our "meaning of money" stories. It is by sharing our experiences in our own words that we convey to them the important money lessons and insights of our lives that are critical to their wise use and management of our wealth.

Because we feel this way, we invite clients to share with us their "meaning of money" stories early in the discovery process. Often we tell them one of ours so they get a better sense of the value of sharing these types of stories. This is a meaning of money story Scott tells:

I grew up on a small dairy farm in northwest New Mexico, one of 12 children. We had a small dairy farm bordering the San Juan River, across from the Navajo reservation. Things were difficult for us financially so we raised most of our own food. We had dairy cows, chickens, pigs, beef cattle, gardens, and orchards, and we were able to provide for ourselves that way. Shoes and clothes, however, posed a real challenge for my parents. Fourteen pairs of feet were a lot to keep in shoes!

One of the many blessings we had was our Uncle Jack, who had a trading post on the Navajo Reservation, where we could buy clothes and shoes wholesale. Each month or so our family went out to the trading post and got the things we needed. A trading post is not exactly Saks Fifth Avenue; it's a store stocked with only the basic things of a rural life, a general store with sheep and goats, and rugs, jewelry, and the like.

Before we went to the trading post, we invariably had a family meeting to decide who would get what. My father was not one to brook any sort of "confusion," as he called it, when we got to the store. I remember when I was 11, I decided that I was due a new pair of shoes, but the family council had decided that I was not going to get a new pair of shoes, and this left me anything but pleased.

I can still remember sitting in the back seat of the car in the driveway, the whole family ready to go, and we couldn't leave because I was throwing a fit. My father stood in the driveway reasoning with me through the open window of the car. Finally, after some minutes of unsuccessfully trying to persuade me to be happy about what I was going to get, he did something unexpected. He lifted up his shoe and laid it on the window seal of the car, then turned it over to show me the bottom. These were his good Sunday shoes and the bottom was totally broken out. There wasn't enough leather left to re-sole them, even if we had had the money,

He looked me straight in the eye and he said, "Scott, we can't afford to buy me new shoes today, and we cannot afford to buy you new shoes either. Do you understand, son?"

Did I ever! In an instant, through the image powerfully conveyed by that single, unforgettable, moment, I understood what money meant in the Farnsworth family that day. That moment was indelible. It still shapes the way I think of money; it's still affects the way I respond when my children ask me for things.

By listening to a dozen or so stories like that from our clients, we start to get an honest, unvarnished sense of what money means to them. Multi-page questionnaires used by traditional advisors can be "gamed," that is, we can answer them in a way that we think we're supposed to answer them. But in the composite telling of a dozen or more meaning of money stories, each client's own truth will emerge. Both we and the clients will know for sure what they want their money to do for them today and in the future, and what they want it to provide for the people and causes for whom they care most deeply. Both we and the clients will know what their plan should do for the *people* involved. Of course, clients may not know the technical steps to take to get to that result—that's our job—but they will understand clearly the future story we're trying to create for them and those they love.

The Life Circle

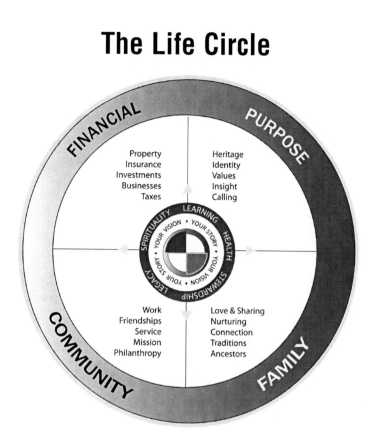

Besides the money, there are lots of other foundational pieces for which we need to hear "meaning of" stories. We sometimes use The Life Circle as a roadmap to help us visit the stories that shed light on these key components of a good plan. Those stories will lead us to answers to questions like "What do you see as your life's purpose, and how did you come to understand what it was?" and "Who do you consider 'family' and what do each of them mean to you?" and "Besides your family, who else is important in your life and why?" and "What causes and organizations do you stand behind and what led you to feel that way?"

As those stories are shared, they lead the clients and us to consider, for each dimension of their lives, another important set of questions: "How do you personally define success in each of these areas of your life?" Once again, the answers reside in the client's stories. Once again, by listening attentively and lovingly to their stories, we can glean the true answers. We can then ask the next questions, the questions at the heart of the matter: "What is still missing for you to feel successful in each dimension of your life and how can we help you achieve it? What are the stories you want to be able to tell about your life's purpose, your family, your community, and your financial well-being, and how can we help make it possible for you to tell them?"

The Life Circle reminds us that all the pieces of life are interrelated; similarly, all the stories are interrelated. A meaning of money story can tell us just as much about the meaning of family or the meaning of community as about the meaning of money. And the same principle applies to financial plans and estate plans: it's never just about the money, because everything we do with the money affects the other pieces. It affects family relationships, it affects our footprint in the communities we care about, and it affects our ability to live our life with purpose.

Story-based planning is meaningful because it helps us understand and then piece together the most important parts of our life in a plan that reflects our deepest values.

Story-based planning is enjoyable.

Story-based planning is more enjoyable than traditional planning because it is collaborative in nature. It is not something the lawyer or financial planner does *to us*, nor is it something they do *for us*; it is something our advisor does *with us*.

Story-based planning requires an advisor who understands that when an advisor and a client sit down together to plan, there are two experts in the room, not just one. The advisor may be the expert on investments, insurance, taxes, legal documents, public benefits, and the like, but the clients are the experts on their life, their stories, their family, and their values. All of the advisor's technical knowledge, which is absolutely critical to the success of the plan, is sadly worthless unless the client's knowledge about their life, story, family, and values is effectively brought into the process and incorporated into every nook and cranny of the plan. Both sets of knowledge must be brought together in a seamless whole or the planning will ultimately fail.

This truth makes it crystal clear that the advisor must bring a second type of knowledge to the table: the knowledge of how to create an environment in which the client can think and speak and share and contribute to the design of the plan as an equal partner with the advisor. Our friend Nancy Kline calls such an environment a Thinking Environment®. She teaches that without a Thinking Environment, the advisor will never be able to create the best possible plan because huge chunks of the solution will remain locked up inside the client. Not only will the advisor not know the answers, he won't even know the questions, that is, the questions he should be asking both himself and the client.

One of the obstacles to a Thinking Environment thrown up by traditional planners is their use of industry jargon, acronyms, and other obtuse language. By contrast, story-based planning is more enjoyable because it is conducted in the language of story rather than in "legalese" or "financial planner-ese" or some other similar language. We've all had the experience of being in a situation where all those around us were speaking a language we didn't understand. We felt uneasy and perhaps ignorant, but certainly inhibited in our ability to contribute. We expect to have such feelings when we're traveling on the other side of the globe, but not when we visit the office of our lawyer or financial advisor.

Story-based planning eliminates these barriers to communication and contribution. When an advisor uses the language of story, it creates a level playing field for the client and invites the client to fully participate in the process.

Peggy has learned that using a story-based approach can make otherwise awkward situations comfortable both for the advisor and the clients. She's also found that it can lead to exceptional ideas and unique solutions that would be unimaginable to advisors not open to working with their clients' stories. She shares this story:

> As a family wealth and legacy counselor I often get the unique opportunity to learn about families in ways they didn't know they were willing to share. I'm fascinated by how amazing each person is. When I combine the insight about each person with their family dynamic, some truly awesome results can be obtained.
>
> Many families approach the estate planning process with the idea that there are only a few ways to accomplish their goals. In our practice, we've found that there are an unlimited number of planning combinations that allow us to co-create plans with our clients; it all depends on their willingness to consider the possibilities, while opening up their hearts and their minds.
>
> I could tell endless stories about how wonderful some of these families are, but one family stands out in particular. I first met the couple at an educational workshop. They were struggling with the assimilation of information to create a plan that would benefit and protect their soon-to-be eighteen year old son who has autism.
>
> Eventually they found their way to my office. To my surprise, they brought their son with them, but it soon became obvious that this was absolutely appropriate as he was really the center and focus of their concerns and need for a cohesive plan. What

caught me off guard the most, however, was that not only were the mother and her husband present, but also the father and his wife! I thought to myself, "This is sure to be an interesting getting-to-know-you exercise."

At first the meeting seemed a little uncomfortable, but before long, everyone began focusing on the object of everyone's affection and the stories started tumbling forth: stories of his birth, of when he was a small child, of his grade school years, and finally his high school experience. The unique bond the four adults shared was based on their love for him.

This young man was absolutely engaging. Very shy at first and wary of my dog, Leiden, who is a constant fixture in my office, it wasn't long before he was adding his own creative element to our dialogue. With a limited command of the English language but with an absolute spark of enthusiasm and humor, he helped our unlikely group share their hopes, fears, dreams, and concerns for creating a whole and fulfilling life for this wonderful young adult.

As a result of their story sharing, the guardian advocacy plan we created together for our young man contemplated the role to be played by each of the biological parents, as well as by the step parents. One step parent will be actively involved, the other will not. The mother and her husband were also able to craft a plan that considered their unique circumstances while providing a special needs trust to be managed by the step father while still incorporating the daily care requirement of the biological father. Each parent's personality and role were clearly reflected in the final plan. I believe this would not have been possible without the benefit of their family stories, revealing personalities, strengths, weaknesses, needs and desires.

I feel a real affection for and closeness to this young man and his family. Our encounters, though brief are intense. To this day, he emails me regularly to keep me apprised of his life and "doings" and he watches Wheel of Fortune for me to make sure my wheel number isn't called and I miss the grand prize. I welcome every opportunity I have to interact with him and cherish this new-found friendship.

If we were to compare the enjoyment this family felt working with Peggy to their likely experience had they gone to a traditional planner, we'd see there's no comparison. Working together, exploring their stories, and combining their collective wisdom, Peggy and this family found the ideal solution to a very challenging human situation.

Ronald Reagan was fond of saying, "You can accomplish almost anything if you don't care who gets the credit." When advisors put their egos aside, listen to their clients and their stories, and invite all to join in the search for answers, the process becomes deeply enjoyable and they find better answers.

Story-based planning is effective.

Besides being more meaningful and more enjoyable, story-based planning delivers better results. A big reason is its collaborative nature, as mentioned above. Another reason is that it opens to view possibilities previously unseen. But perhaps most importantly, it assures that the client and the advisor are asking the right questions. We have learned that when you ask the wrong questions, you almost always end up with the wrong answers.

One of the wrong questions that traditional planners often ask, when exposed to story-based planning is, "Doesn't it take too long?" The question itself speaks volumes about the traditional planner's mind-set. The reality is that story-based planning doesn't take much more time than traditional planning, but that's beside the point. When it comes to something this important to our individual and family happiness, *effectiveness* is what matters most, not *efficiency*. Racing a thousand miles an hour in the wrong direction may feel productive, but it's really only taking us further away from our goal faster. "Sometimes with people, slow is fast and fast is slow." (Stephen R. Covey)

Another way traditional planners frequently end up with the wrong answers is by focusing too narrowly on the numbers, especially numbers with dollar signs in front of them. Don't get us wrong, we care as deeply about the dollars as anyone. But we believe that other questions are even more important. Financial authors Scott West and Mitch Anthony pose one example in their book, *Your Client's Story:* "After all, in the long run, what is more important, the money we leave or the messages we leave with it?" For us and most clients we've worked with, the answer to that and several similar questions is obvious.

Columnist Ellen Goodman described recently what she and most of the people we've worked with really want from estate planning "What we really want from the generations past are not just the facts or the DNA. We want the stories. Love, passion, successes, disappointment, humanity. . . . [H]ow many of us would trade in the data for one good diary? Will we remember that in our own 'estate planning'"?

Story-based planning asks the right questions, which leads to better answers. Shortly after moving to the Orlando area about a decade ago, Scott worked with a client who faced several difficult planning challenges. Using story-based planning, Scott and his colleagues were able to achieve an outstanding outcome, not only for the client but for many other people he cared about. In telling this story, we have changed the names and certain non-material details to preserve the client's confidentiality.

Mr. Jacobs came to see our firm when he was 88 years old. With an estate worth approximately $9 million, he was looking down the barrel of an estate tax of about $5 million, largely because of some botched planning that had previously been done for him.

After reviewing the situation, I asked Mr. Jacobs if he were open to the idea of charitable giving. He was. "I've been a lifelong member of Rotary, and I'd be happy to donate $2,000. My deceased wife was an active member of a sewing club. I could give them $3,000 in her memory."

I decided to save the discussion of charitable giving for another time. Instead, I started getting to know Mr. Jacobs. He was a good man with a remarkable story. It seems he had grown up and spent his long life on two pieces of ground. Born in upstate New York, he had lived on a farm there until his family moved when he was 10. They bought a small farm near the town of Ocoee, where he had lived ever since.

He'd certainly had his share of misfortune. As a boy in New York, he had lost an eye in a farming accident. He also had been afflicted with polio, so one of his legs was withered, and he walked with a pronounced limp. He had been married for many years, but his wife had passed away about five years before I met him. He had one child, a daughter in her mid-50's who had not fulfilled any particular ambitions, and still waited tables at a local all-you-can-eat restaurant. She had two children, a son and a daughter, both in their early 20's at the time. Both were heavily involved with illicit drug use. The son had been arrested for dealing drugs for his father, Mr. Jacobs' ex-son-in-law, who was serving time in a federal prison. Mr. Jacobs' granddaughter was also pregnant; Mr. Jacobs did not know who the father might be

In view of all this, and understandably, while Mr. Jacobs wanted to make sure that his child's and his grandchildren's needs were met, he certainly had no intention of leaving them $9 million. Mr. Jacobs had worked hard all his life. When he was a teenager, he and his father had built a service station on their property, which Mr. Jacobs had operated since he was 18. He told me interesting stories about sleeping in the station all night, so in case a car drove by, he would be there to sell them a quarter's worth of gas. At one point, he owned his own tanker truck, and worked in the station all day, and drove a tanker to Tampa, which in those days, took four or five hours, filled up, drove back, and worked all day taking care of customers.

Ocoee, where Mr. Jacobs lived, might fairly be described as a stepchild of Orange County—a town with a hard luck story much like Mr. Jacobs'. In the early 1920's, there had been a race riot there on Election Day. Several people were killed—an incident that had stigmatized the town and still cast a shadow over it even these many years later. Early in the Great Depression, the town lost its bank, leaving it no source of lending for businesses looking to put down roots and grow there. Mr. Jacobs told me that he knew a number of merchants who went to the bank of a nearby town seeking a loan, and were refused because the bank did not want to support businesses that would compete with those in its own town.

Mr. Jacobs chose to use this setback as an opportunity. In the 1960's, he and a few Rotary Club buddies opened a bank in Ocoee. His capital contribution was the land on which the bank was built. One merger followed another until eventually Mr. Jacobs' investment of land for the bank had returned the current value of his estate—$9 million.

Mr. Jacobs and I spent a good bit of time together. I helped him capture and articulate some of these stories. I wanted to make sure that, in addition to protecting the financial resources he had, we also preserved the rest of his wealth—who he was, what he had learned, and the values that had guided him to his hard-won wisdom, and ensure that these somehow would be passed along intact to those who would follow him, even though, at the time, they did not seem particularly interested in what he had to say.

As we talked one afternoon, I was struck by an insight into what might be important for Mr. Jacobs. He was describing his friendships and associations with citizens of Ocoee, his adopted hometown, and it suddenly seemed clear to me that this was the key. "Mr. Jacobs," I asked, "what would you think if we could take the money in your estate that otherwise would go to the IRS, and instead direct it into an account that you and those you trust could dispense for projects in Ocoee?"

He looked at me and asked, "What do you mean?"

"We could take the money that otherwise would have to be paid in taxes, and see to it that it was spent to improve the town and the lives of the people there."

He was intrigued. "Give me an example," he said, leaning forward.

"Well," I said, "suppose that the elementary school needed new playground equipment. We could take some of the money that we had set aside in a special fund—one that you and those you trust could control—and buy the equipment. If the girls needed a new softball field to play on, you could finance its construction. If you just wanted to make the Christmas parade extra special one year, you could direct funds to do just that."

Mr. Jacobs's eyes grew wide; I could see he was imagining the possibilities. "We could do that?" he asked.

"Indeed, we could. And it wouldn't take away anything from your family, because the money we'd be using to set up the fund would otherwise just have gone to the government."

Mr. Jacobs sat back in his chair with a deeply satisfied grin. "This is exciting," he said, and a new mood of enthusiasm came over him. He was already planning what he would do with the money.

Rather than giving $2,000 to the Rotary Club or $3,000 to his wife's sewing circle, Mr. Jacobs ended up contributing $5 million. The money was used, as we had discussed, to create a fund to benefit the city of Ocoee—a fund that would be controlled by him and those he trusted, and be used expressly to support worthwhile community projects for that town, in keeping with the things that Mr. Jacobs felt were most important. With his wife gone, and appropriate arrangements made to care for his child and grandchildren, his remaining great love was the town of Ocoee. The difference that this advising made for him and for the citizens of Ocoee may well extend beyond the foreseeable future, benefiting countless generations to come.

Using Mr. Jacobs' case as a model for what can be accomplished using story-based planning, what are some of the results we can expect to see from this approach?

In this example, we can see a number of results that can be calculated in numbers. The number of tax dollars saved was in the millions. The number of dollars directed to a very worthy cause was likewise in the millions. Mr. Jacobs' family received a substantial sum, according to their needs. Although not mentioned in this account, the plan bypassed much of the probate process, thus saving many months and many thousands of dollars of expenses when Mr. Jacobs passed away. Measured by numbers alone, the results were outstanding.

But some of the most important outcomes cannot be calculated in dollars and cents or measured in numbers. These are the human results, which we believe are far more important than the numerical ones. For Mr. Jacobs himself, the results were stunning. Because of our use of a story-based process, Mr. Jacobs felt heard and understood. He was able to participate actively in the design of his plan. He was able to share his lifetime of amazing stories and save them for a time in the future when his family would want to hear them. He was able to identify the causes he felt passionate about, causes that had not previously been obvious to him. He found new energy and new purpose in his life, as he saw his plan come together and then play out before his eyes. He found a peace of mind that had eluded him before, a peace of mind based on reviewing his life, putting together its pieces, and then fashioning a legacy that would allow him to know that he had made a difference in the lives of those for whom he cared most.

The results for others are equally profound and valuable. The town of Ocoee will be blessed for many years to come by the gifts that will come from Mr. Jacobs' foundation. This in turn will create a new pride for the town, and will likely result in a higher quality of life for all its citizens. Mr. Jacobs' planning may be the inspiration for others to do the same, thus blessing their lives and the causes they choose to support. Those who administer Mr. Jacobs' foundation will be touched by the trust and confidence Mr. Jacobs showed in them. They will also be uplifted by the opportunity to identify needs in the community and then direct resources to address those needs. Mr. Jacobs' family will have their material needs met through Mr. Jacobs' planning, but they will also be nourished by his stories and encouraged by his example of hard work, integrity, ingenuity, loyalty, and generosity. The list of potential benefits and beneficiaries goes on and on.

Story-based planning is perhaps most effective in helping clients identify and build their legacy, which we define not as statues of ourselves or buildings with our names on them, but the impact we have on the people and causes we care about most. "What you leave behind is not what is engraved in stone monuments, but what is woven into the lives of others." (Pericles) The question of legacy arises from a deep yearning we all have to have made a difference during our time on the planet.

At the center of our being there really are things we have a huge desire to do or accomplish. We keep putting those things off because we live in a frenetic, busy world and tend to spend most of our time reacting to the demands of external influences, other people, financial problems, physical ailments, and so on. . . . Life's real fulfillment comes when we honestly answer these questions: What really matters most to me? What would I really like to accomplish? What legacy would I like to leave behind? (Hyrum Smith, *What Matters Most*)

Dr. Ernest Becker, a Pulitzer Prize-winning psychologist who specialized in the care of the terminally ill, wrote in his book *The Denial of Death*: "What man really fears is not so much extinction but extinction with insignificance. Man wants to know that his life has somehow counted, if not for himself, then at least in the larger scheme of things, that it has left a trace, a trace that has meaning."

We found the topic of legacy to be somewhat nebulous to clients until we began to use a graphic model we call The Legacy Circle. The Legacy Circle helps clients appreciate that a well-designed legacy plan provides for several components woven into a unified tapestry.

The Legacy Circle

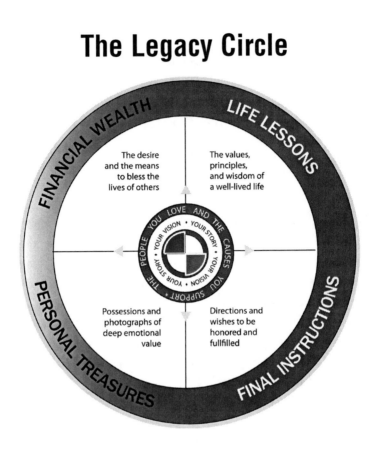

A large part of legacy is a compilation of our life lessons, including the values, principles, and wisdom acquired during our time on earth. These lessons, which can be passed down in a variety of ways, are best conveyed in our stories, for all the reasons outlined in this book. We teach best by sharing stories, which allow our messages to touch the hearts of our listeners. So the best way to impart our life-lessons to others is through our stories. A legacy plan without stories is like a car without a motor and wheels—not likely to get very far.

Directions and wishes to be honored and fulfilled, or final instructions, provide clarity for loved ones as we approach the end of life. Such requests are more likely to be carried out if they are couched within the personal narratives of our lives when such matters became important to us. For example, if one of our final instructions is our wish that our son go back to college and graduate, he will be more inclined to do so if he hears our personal experiences in our own words about the value of a college education and diploma.

As we have seen, personal treasures such as keepsakes and photographs have greater value to others and are more likely to be cherished when they remain connected with our stories about them. Interestingly, the same is true regarding our financial wealth; with our stories it can accomplish far more good for the recipients than a pile of money without the messages.

There are many sources of help in designing and passing on our legacies. Personal and family historians, videographers, scrapbookers, genealogists, ethical will drafters, and others in related fields can help us share and save our stories, and we applaud them for their work. But to create a comprehensive and effective legacy plan, we think one of the key members of the Legacy Builder team needs to be a story-based financial advisor or estate planner. Such advisors have the unique capability of integrating the money with the non-financial components of the legacy, which will have the effect of magnifying the impact of each. We think there are significant advantages of working with a story-based financial advisor and estate planner as essential members of a legacy planning team.

What to Look for in an Advisor

Developing a financial services or estate planning practice that is driven by a story-based planning process requires a different breed of professional advisor. What should a client be looking for in such an advisor? What does it take for a professional to work successfully in this model? In our experience, effective story-based advisors need four things besides the technical capabilities that are standard for their profession.

They should have a new mind-set, a new skill-set, a new tool-set, and a new support-set.

Successful story-based advisors need a mind-set different from the one they acquired in law school, business school, or insurance company training. They still need outstanding technical skills, but they also need to understand the power and importance of story. They need to "get it" that real human communication and connection happen far more effectively (and efficiently) in a story, rather than in a spreadsheet. They must love hearing and telling stories. They must value the human dimensions of true wealth and not be narrowly focused on the numbers or the dollar signs.

They also need a skill-set that is markedly different from that of traditional planners. They need to be incredibly good listeners who hear not only the words spoken by their clients but also the meanings between the lines and in the pauses and cadences of their clients' voices. They must be drivingly curious to know what their clients really think and really feel and really want to achieve in their work together. They must see their clients as their equals in their thinking capabilities, and as their superiors as holders of their own life stories. They must be skilled at creating an environment where stories and other kinds of thinking can flourish consistently. They must be able to catch the visions their clients see, and then use their technical skills (or those of their planning teams) to put a foundation under those dreams and build them into reality.

This new breed of advisors needs a new tool-set to be able to work effectively and efficiently in this exciting new model of planning. They need a stockpile of their own stories so they can show clients how to share and connect in this way. They need a supply of story-leading questions to spark the stories in their clients' memories. They need recorders to capture and preserve the stories they hear that are intended to be included as part of the plan and passed forward to future generations. They need presentations so they can spread the story-based planning message to small groups and large audiences.

We use a wide array of tools in our Legacy Builder work. Some of the specific tools we use with our clients are a family of story-based chats called Priceless Conversations. These tool kits provide the information, the process, and the deliverables we need for a series of 30-60 minute-long interviews on a wide variety of legacy topics. Some topics, such as "The Meaning of Money," "The Meaning of Success," or "My Plan," are specifically designed to help clients get clear about what they want in their planning; to help us better understand our clients so we can design a more effective plan; and, at the same time, to create a recording of important stories to be added to what we call their "Legacy Library." Other Priceless Conversations make it comfortable and convenient for them to tell stories and leave messages for and about their children, their spouses, their children with handicaps or special needs, their adopted children, or their pets. Still other Priceless Conversations invite them to share and save stories about the "Angels and Heroes" in their lives, their home places, their keepsakes, their war experiences, their wishes for the last chapters of their life, and their wisdom and life-lessons. These Priceless Conversation Tool Kits make it easy and affordable for us to create lasting treasures for our clients and their loved ones.

In addition to a new mind-set, a new skill-set, and a new tool-set, advisors using a story-based model of planning need a new support-set. It's not easy being a trail blazer. There's an old saying out West that seems to apply here: "You can always tell the true pioneers; they're the ones with the arrows in their backs." Until such time as this model of planning becomes the norm (and we see that happening in the very near future as the general population becomes aware of it and its many advantages), a lot of these pioneering planners are affiliated with the SunBridge Legacy Builder Network. It helps them get outfitted and then stay equipped for the journey. For clients and prospective clients who don't already have a qualified story-based financial advisor or estate planner, we think it's an excellent place to locate one.

We believe story-based planning has the potential to quietly but dramatically improve the world by touching hearts, connecting families, and changing lives. We think that within a few years, this will be the only way thoughtful people will even consider planning. We look forward to that day with excitement and anticipation. ∞

CHAPTER 8

SHARING YOUR STORIES AND COMING ALIVE

"DON'T ASK YOURSELF
WHAT THE WORLD NEEDS;
ASK YOURSELF WHAT
MAKES YOU COME ALIVE.
AND THEN GO AND DO THAT.
BECAUSE WHAT THE WORLD
NEEDS IS PEOPLE WHO
HAVE COME ALIVE."
— HAROLD WHITMAN

Harold Whitman's advice is not intended just to benefit the world; it is especially intended to benefit each of us. Discovering what makes us come alive is a quest worthy of our best efforts because it will transform us and change the world.

When we know what makes us come alive, we discover boundless energy, passion, and purpose doing whatever *it* is. When we know what makes us come alive, we help more, we share more, and we give more of ourselves—because there is more of us to give. When we know what makes us come alive, we see the world not as a vale of tears but as a field of opportunity; we see others not as objects or obstacles, but as fellow human travelers who deserve our finest service on their behalf.

In *Pygmalion*, George Bernard Shaw was speaking as one who had come alive when he wrote:

> This is the true joy in life—being used for a purpose recognized by yourself as a mighty one; being thoroughly worn out before you are thrown on the scrap heap; being a force of nature instead of feverish, selfish little clod of ailments and grievances complaining that the world will not devote itself to making you happy.
>
> I am of the opinion that my life belongs to the whole community and as long as I live, it is my privilege to do for it whatever I can.
>
> I want to be thoroughly used up when I die, for the harder I work, the more I live. I rejoice in life for its own sake. Life is no "brief candle" to me. It is a sort of splendid torch which I have got hold of for the moment, and I want to make it burn as brightly as possible before handing it on to future generations.

How, one may ask, can we come to know what makes us come alive? How can we uncover a nugget of such value, a pearl of such great price? The answer, we think, is to be found within the world of stories. In the process of sifting through our life experiences to create stories, or as we share them with someone else, or perhaps as we listen to the tales of another, we will find the key that opens the door that leads to the place inside us where we will recognize the cause that makes us want to "work harder" and "rejoice in life" and "be thoroughly used up when we die."

Of all the incredible benefits we get from stories, this may be the ultimate: they guide us to discover what makes us come alive.

Once we are alive with meaning and purpose, our impact and influence on others is magnified, regardless of our place in the world and regardless of our station in life. "Let no man imagine he has no influence. Whoever he may be, and wherever he may be placed, the man who thinks becomes a light and a power." (Henry George)

In recounting his story of a brief encounter with a college lacrosse player, Robert Feisee of Ashburn, Virginia, discovered the spark that drives him to seek to influence others for good regardless of how long or in what way he may be in their presence. He shares this story:

I sometimes wonder how my life might have turned out if I had not met Frank.

I love the sport of lacrosse but I grew up and went to high school in northern Virginia where lacrosse was not even a varsity sport, rather it was a club activity. Because of that, I figured that I had little chance to play in college or to even get the opportunity to be seen by a college team.

After my junior year in high school, I spent the summer running a beach stand in Ocean City, Maryland. After work I would join pick-up volleyball games on the beach just to have something to do. During one of those games I happened to be wearing my high school club lacrosse shorts that bore the logo "Bruins Lacrosse." After the game, one of the players asked me if I played lacrosse for the Brown University Bruins. I said, "No, although I'd love to play there someday."

Frank introduced himself and said he played lacrosse at Cornell University. I was excited to be actually talking to a real college player and I think Frank could sense my excitement. He asked if I wanted to "throw around" the next afternoon and I eagerly accepted.

The next day, I met Frank after work in front of a condo that had a small patch of grass. He asked me about where I played and how I got started in the game. He took a keen interest in what I had to say and treated me almost like he was my big brother. By the way he listened to me I could tell he genuinely cared about what happened to me even though we had just met.

We started throwing the ball around and he was really good. He showed me a technique and a few moves that a specialty position would use at what is called the "face-off." He told me how I could practice the technique and get very good at it. After about 15 minutes, he had to leave for a previous commitment.

I never saw Frank again, but I practiced his technique all summer. In my senior year, I used the technique that Frank taught me and received high local honors. In the spring I was accepted at Syracuse University, and that fall I decided to try out for their varsity lacrosse team as a walk-on.

All my friends thought I was crazy because Syracuse was the defending national champion, but I believed I could play there because I had been taught by someone who played at Cornell. Frank's lessons and my subsequent success using what he had taught me had generated a confidence within me that was hard to describe. Besides sharing techniques and moves, he had helped me visualize my goal of playing lacrosse in college, a dream that just a year earlier had seemed so far away.

Seventy very good players tried out for 35 slots on the Syracuse varsity lacrosse team that fall. Most of them had much more experience than I did, but I happened to be one of the long shots who made it. Over the next four years, I had an incredible experience playing at Syracuse. While I was there, our team won two more national championships.

I treasure my time at Syracuse and the camaraderie with the other players, and the two championship rings are a nice addition to my library as well. But I'm not telling this story to brag about myself or the team. Instead, my purpose is to give credit to Frank and to demonstrate that one person *can* make a huge difference in another person's life simply by giving them 15 minutes of their time and attention.

The confidence I learned from Frank not only helped me in the sport of lacrosse, it was also the inspiration that guided me to pass the CFP exam, finish law school, and set up my own business. I ask myself again, I wonder how my life might have turned out if I had not met Frank.

I now coach a high school lacrosse team, and I use stories a lot as a coach. I have some great lacrosse stories from playing for an outstanding collegiate team and competing for two national championships. But the most important story I have is about a generous player from Cornell who changed the life of a star-struck 16-year-old with 15 minutes of attention and a few lacrosse pointers. When I meet a young man who questions his ability to compete successfully, whether in lacrosse or some other part of life, I try to pass on to him everything Frank gave me that summer afternoon in Ocean City while we were just "throwing around." My mission is to be the "Frank" in some other young man's life.

We love Robert's story because it points out that "coming alive" doesn't necessarily require an earth-shattering, jaw-dropping mission. We have noticed, however, that it almost always involves having a passion or purpose for helping others, and it invariably demands the very best of us. Or perhaps it is the case that once we discover what it is that makes us come alive, we demand the very best of ourselves in carrying it out.

We live in the Orlando area and we see daily the impact of one single person who came alive as perhaps no 20th Century American ever did. Walt Disney was alive with energy, creativity, and a sense of mission and purpose as he brought to reality his vision of "Walt Disney World." Now, nearly 50 years since the story of the grandest of all family vacation destinations sparked his imagination, nearly 50 million people a year are touched by Disney's magic. That dream drove him and filled him with life right up to the very end.

Mike Vance, former dean of Disney University, tells this story of Walt Disney's final hours in 1966:

At Disney studios in Burbank, California, Mike could gaze out of his office window across Buena Vista Street to St. Joseph's Hospital, where Walt Disney died. Mike was talking on the telephone when he saw the flag being lowered over the hospital around 8:20 a.m. His death was preceded by an amazing incident that reportedly took place the night before in Walt's hospital room.

A journalist, knowing Walt was seriously ill, persisted in getting an interview with Walt and was frustrated on numerous occasions by the hospital staff. When he finally managed to get into the room, Walt couldn't sit up in bed or talk above a whisper. Walt instructed the reporter to lie down on the bed, next to him, so he could whisper in the reporter's ear. For the next 30 minutes, Walt and the journalist lay side by side as Walt referred to an imaginary map of Walt Disney World on the ceiling above the bed.

Walt pointed out where he planned to place various attractions and buildings. He talked about transportation, hotels, restaurants, and many other parts of his vision for a property that wouldn't open to the public for another six years.

We told this reporter's moving experience, relayed through a nurse, to our organizational development groups, . . . the story of how a man who lay dying in the hospital whispered in the reporter's ear for 30 minutes, describing his vision for the future and the role he would play in it for generations to come.

This is the way to live—believing so much in your vision that even when you're dying, you whisper it into another person's ear.

Soon after the completion of The Magic Kingdom at Walt Disney World, someone said, "Isn't it too bad Walt Disney didn't live to see this?" Vance replied, "He did see it. That's why it's here." (Mike Vance and Diane Deacon, *Think Out of the Box)*

So what is it that makes you come alive? What is it that will inspire *you,* like Walt Disney, to whisper it into another person's ear even when you're dying? And where in your stories will you discover it?

Then once you know what it is, what will your new story be? Who will you be in that new story and what will the world look like once you, like Walt Disney, work your magic upon it? We challenge you to dream big and tell big stories, stories worthy of your greatness. ∽

CHAPTER 9

FIND YOUR STORY AND MAKE IT HAPPEN

"LET US ENDEAVOR TO LIVE
SO THAT WHEN WE COME
TO DIE EVEN THE UNDERTAKER
WILL BE SORRY."

—MARK TWAIN

In previous chapters, we have seen the power and versatility of stories. We have discovered countless benefits, large and small, from sharing and saving them. It might be helpful to remind ourselves of a few of those benefits. We think the list is pretty impressive.

- Stories cradle the wisdom and learning of a lifetime.
- Stories define our uniqueness.
- Stories confirm our shared humanity.
- Stories keep us alive in the lives and hearts of others.
- Stories allow us to have a greater influence in the lives of others.
- Stories help us make important decisions.
- Stories foster feelings of closeness and affection.
- Stories renew old relationships effortlessly and fire up new relationships quickly.
- Stories help us appreciate our strengths and overcome our challenges.
- Stories allow us to see the world through another's eyes.

- Stories make it possible for us to assimilate and manage vast amounts of information.
- Stories serve as a buffer to the raw events of life.
- Stories help us discover our deepest values.
- Stories help us mend broken relationships.
- Stories facilitate life review and help us put life events in perspective.
- Stories create order and a sense of flow in our lives.
- Stories act as an antidote to the shallowness of modern life.
- Stories begin the process of personal healing.
- Stories slow the mindless pace of modern life.
- Stories open an emotional connection between the teller and the listener.
- Stories rescue us from hopelessness and despair.
- Stories help us see larger possibilities for our lives.
- Stories draw others to us, and us to others.
- Stories bind families together over generations.
- Stories are our ticket to immortality.
- Stories are love gifts.
- Stories make our feelings of loss a little easier to handle.
- Stories transmit family values—without preaching or moralizing.
- Stories keep alive the people who lived them.
- Stories turn keepsakes and photographs into priceless treasures.
- Stories draw us back to our faith.
- Stories bring home places to life.
- Stories create better financial planning and estate planning.
- Stories allow us and our advisors to get an honest, unvarnished sense of what money, success, family, community, and other important matters mean to us.
- Stories eliminate barriers to communication and contribution.
- Stories unveil previously unseen solutions.
- Stories lead us to ask the right questions.
- Stories help us find what makes us come alive.

So now, what are we to do with what we know? How do we personally benefit from this list of potential benefits?

Fortunately, there's one other attribute of stories that may prove to be very handy in this situation: **stories touch us and inspire us and move us to action.** The right story can get us up off the couch and propel us into motion. The right story can drive us to push through obstacles and adversities, hardships and handicaps. The right story can get us going. That means that all we have to do is find the right story, the one that moves *us* to action, and we're on our way!

We wrote this book because we found a story that brings us alive. In our story, we see thousands, maybe millions, inspired to recall the stories of their childhood, their youth, and their old age; of their days at school, in the service, and on the job; of their families, friends, and colleagues; of the triumphs and tragedies, the sadness and celebrations of their lives. We see these people sharing stories of courage, inspiration, hope, faith, and love with children, grandchildren, friends, and advisors. We see their stories touching hearts, connecting families, and changing lives. We see ourselves changing the world, one story at a time.

Our fondest hope is that each of our readers will also be moved to action—to find the story that brings them alive, to live their story fully with passion and purpose, and to share their story with those they love. ∽

ABOUT THE AUTHORS

SCOTT FARNSWORTH is an attorney and a Certified Financial Planner©. He is the president of SunBridge, Inc. and the founder of The Legacy Builder Network. He is the author of *Closing the Gap: A Revolutionary Approach to Client Services.*

Scott was recently named one of *Financial Advisor Magazine's* "Innovators of the Year." He designs and delivers transformative workshops for professionals, including *"The Legacy Builder Retreat," "Less Selling—More Sales,"* and *"The Wealth & Wisdom Summit."*

He is the inventor of The SunBridge Money & Success Client Connection System, and is a certified Time to Think Coach and Consultant.

Scott is a native of Fruitland, New Mexico. He earned his undergraduate degree *magna cum laude* in Portuguese and Political Science and his law degree *magna cum laude* from Brigham Young University. During law school he was the Managing Editor of the Law Review, and published two scholarly articles. Following graduation, he was appointed Judicial Clerk for Paul H. Roney, Circuit Judge for the United States Court of Appeals for the Fifth Circuit.

He has nearly three decades of professional experience as an estate planning attorney, was Vice President and Trust Officer at Trustmark National Bank, and was an assistant professor of business law at the University of Southern Mississippi. He and his wife Marcie live in Harmony, Florida, and are the parents of six children.

To contact Scott, please call 407-593-2386 or visit www.SunBridgeLegacy.com or www.CertifiedLegacyAdvisor.com.

PEGGY HOYT is an attorney. She and her law partner, Randy Bryan, are the founders of Hoyt & Bryan, LLC, an estate planning firm located in Oviedo, Florida, dedicated to family wealth and legacy counseling. She is a nationally recognized public speaker and has authored a number of books on unique estate planning topics including: *All My Children Wear Fur Coats—How to Leave a Legacy for Your Pet; Special People, Special Planning—Creating a Safe Legal Haven for Families with Special Needs; Loving Without a License—An Estate Planning Survival Guide for Unmarried Couples and Same Sex Partners; A Matter of Trust— The Importance of Personal Instructions;* and *Women in Transition—Navigating the Legal and Financial Transitions in Your Life.*

Peggy is a native of Dearborn, Michigan. Her degrees include a B.B.A *cum laude*, M.B.A, and J.D. *cum laude*, all from Stetson University. Before attending law school, she provided investment advice and assistance as a financial consultant for Merrill Lynch. Peggy is active in both the local and national professional estate planning community including the Central Florida Estate Planning Council, Sunbridge, WealthCounsel, InKnowVision and the National Network of Estate Planning Attorneys.

Peggy's passion is her pets (all 13 of them), but especially her horses with whom she does long distance trail riding. She lives with her husband Joe in Chuluota, Florida.

To contact Peggy, please call **407-977-8080** or visit **www.HoytBryan.com**. Her books are available through her firm or her website.

CONTRIBUTORS

Robert A. Feisee
Robert A. Feisee, JD, CFP®
44365 Premier Plaza, Suite 220
Ashburn, VA 20147
703-654-6019
raf@raf-law.com
www.wealthlaw.net

Steve Gammill
Jan Gammill
J. Stephen Gammill, LLC
P.O. Box 190, 849 Celestite Dr.
Fruita, CO 81521
970-858-9135
stevegammill@bresnan.net
jangammill@bresnan.net
www.Stevegammill.com

Bradley L. Hahn PC
Bradley L. Hahn, Counsellor
 & Attorney at Law
4500 S. Lakeshore Drive, Suite 480
Tempe, AZ 85282
480-627-2444
brad@bradleylhahn.com
www.bradleylhahn.com

Mary Lou James CFP
SWP Group LLC
40 SW 12th Street, Ste 102A
Ocala, FL 34471
352-690-6116
mljames@swpgroup.net
www.strategicwealthpartners.com

Jeffrey Knapp
The Knapp Law Firm LLC
11 South Finley Ave.
Basking Ridge, NJ 07920
908-696-0011
jknapp@knapplaw.net
www.knapplaw.net

Robert Kwiatkowski
Merrill Lynch
6807 Hampton Creek Way
Springfield, VA 22150
703-507-6089
robert_kwiatkowski@ml.com
http://fa.ml.com/robert_kwiatkowski

Benjamin Light
Development Director
The Gathering Place
23300 Commerce Park
Cleveland, OH 44122
(216) 595-9546
light@touchedbycancer.org
www.touchedbycancer.org

Chris Mares
Chris J. Mares, S.C.
2210 E. Evergreen Drive
Appleton, WI 54913
920-734-7000
chris@chrismares.com
www.chrismares.com

Darlynn Morgan
Morgan Law Group
4590 MacArthur Blvd. #220
Newport Beach, CA 92660
949-260-1400
info@morganlawgroup.com
www.morganlawgroup.com

Ted Ripley
Estate Planning and Family
 Wealth Preservation
618 S. Peabody St., Suite C
Port Angeles, WA 98362
360-457-0451
ripleylaw@olympus.net

Gary R. Waitzman
Law Offices of Gary R. Waitzman, LLC
250 Parkway Drive, Suite130
Lincolnshire, IL 60069
847-793-1300
gary@grweplaw.com
www.grweplaw.com

LaVergne, TN USA
22 October 2009
161742LV00002B/1/P